The Successful Middle School

This We Believe

Penny A. Bishop, Ed.D.
Lisa M. Harrison, Ph.D.

Association for Middle Level Education

Printed in the United States of America.

Citation

Bishop, P.A. & Harrison, L.M. (2021). *The successful middle school: This we believe.* Association for Middle Level Education.

Stephanie Simpson, CEO
April Tibbles, Editor
Dawn Williams, Designer

ISBN: 978-1-56090-304-8

Library of Congress Control Number: 2020945345

Association for Middle Level Education
2550 Corporate Exchange Dr., Suite 324
Columbus, Ohio 43231 | amle.org

TABLE OF CONTENTS

Dream Big by Mohammed A., Grade 7

*In this drawing I made the character dreaming about his future and what he will do.
He has big dreams and is always positive about doing the best he can to achieve his
goal in life. He wants to make his school and family very proud so he can make a name
for himself.*

Introduction

As this edition of the foundational position paper of the Association for Middle Level Education is being published, our communities face a global pandemic that has closed many school buildings, and we have witnessed racial and social injustices that have shined a light on the inequities that middle school students around the world face on a daily basis.

Despite this adversity, I have seen countless examples of the power of middle school educators to make profound and positive impacts on their students' lives and on their futures. While these times may be uncertain, what is clear is that middle school educators are successful when they focus on creating strong relationships with students and building school environments that are responsive and guided by the distinctive nature and identities of young adolescents. The essential principles first published in this paper nearly 40 years ago remain as relevant and as important as ever.

As stated in this paper, "Vision is an acute sense of the possible." I invite you to commit to building middle schools that are responsive, challenging, empowering, equitable, and engaging. I invite you to honor, respect, and value our young adolescents and to be the adult advocate that helps them wrestle with big ideas and the ups and downs of life. And most importantly, I invite you to join us in imagining what is possible for our students, our school communities, and the world that surrounds them.

Stephanie Simpson
CEO

The First Day

By Roya P., Grade 6

That first day

Where the hall is crowded and loud

You're all alone

And you just want to find a place

Where you can belong

And be yourself

Where you aren't worrying

If what you say, or do, or look like is enough

But this time, that never happened

Because today,

Even though the hall is still crowded and loud

And you don't know anyone here

At this school, people care

No one is afraid to greet you

To show you around

Give you a smile

And show that there is a place for you

Because

You

Are

enough

The Importance of Middle Level Education

The middle school years are an exciting time, as young adolescents are in the midst of profound personal change and identity development. They are growing physically, intellectually, morally, psychologically, and socio-emotionally. They are thinking more deeply about who they are in relation to their race, ethnicity, social class, gender, sexual orientation, religion, and other identities. They are beginning to ponder some of the quintessential questions of life.

Every day, these diverse middle schoolers develop as they engage with the world around them. They socialize with peers and interact with their families and caregivers. They encounter new decisions and make complex life choices. They consume media and express themselves creatively. Along the way, they construct the attitudes, values, and dispositions that will form who they become as adults. Each of these moments is a learning opportunity and the stakes are high; young adolescents' personal development and academic growth during these middle grades years can dramatically impact their futures.[1] The quality of students' middle school experience substantially affects their overall sense of well-being[2] and, in particular, their later chances for high school completion and post-secondary success.[3] Creating successful middle schools, then, is crucial for both individuals and society at large. But what is a successful middle school?

Successful middle schools are responsive. They respond to the nature of young adolescents in all their amazing diversity and are designed specifically to support the developmental needs and social identities of students. Educators and administrators view students in a positive way, rejecting the deficit perspective too often foisted on middle schoolers by society. They are critically conscious of the fact that students' multiple and intersecting identities influence their experiences, opportunities, and perspectives. Therefore, their practices and policies are just and equitable. Teachers build relationships, design curriculum, and create learning environments that support, affirm, and celebrate young adolescents holistically. They expect and plan for a range of capacities and idiosyncratic change, both within and across youth.[4] Such educators know that designing programs on the assumption that every student is ready to become proficient in specific skills at the same time is unrealistic and counterproductive. Instead, teachers offer abundant and meaningful opportunities for each young adolescent to grow, develop an appetite for learning, and acquire needed skills and knowledge. Knowing that students' needs change over time, they offer supportive and scaffolded opportunities for learners to try new things and to make mistakes and learn from them.

Research is clear that not all youth have the same access to responsive middle schools that lay a foundation for success. Learners from historically marginalized groups disproportionately suffer the harmful consequences of bias, discrimination, and systemic oppression.[5] These inequities exist both within and across schools. Latinx and Black students are more likely than students from other racial/ethnic groups to attend under-resourced schools.[6] Students of color are more likely than their White counterparts to experience inequitable and adverse disciplinary actions in school, such as in- and out-of-school suspensions and expulsions.[7] And lesbian, gay, bisexual and transgender (LGBTQ) students have less access to resources and support and are at a higher risk of victimization than their non-LGBTQ peers.[8] To achieve truly responsive middle schools, educators recognize these inequities and implement practices and policies to redress and disrupt them. Their practices and policies justly ensure that each student feels socially connected and valued, becomes competent and skilled, and develops independence and responsibility.

All young adolescents deserve schools that help them become competent and confident individuals who feel a sense of agency, are proud of who they are, are optimistic about their future, feel connected to those around them, and are prepared to succeed in our ever-changing world. In such schools, students pose significant and challenging questions for which there may not be one right answer. They become actively aware of the larger world and how their identities influence their position in it. Students develop the skills and dispositions to understand and embrace diverse perspectives, experiences, and backgrounds different from their own, as well as to question their own belief systems. They learn to think critically, pursue skills and knowledge deeply, and communicate their thoughts clearly with their local and global communities. And they engage in active citizenship by participating in endeavors that serve and benefit those communities, such as exploring more socially just and ecologically sustainable ways of living.

How do we create such responsive and equitable schools? What is the nature of the school's culture and climate? What kinds of curriculum and teaching strategies are most effective? And how are such schools organized and led? These questions—the subject of how to best educate young adolescents in general and indeed the focus of this position paper—have been debated for well over a century. The creation of the first "junior high school" in the U.S. in the early 1900s was an attempt to keep these learners engaged and in school.[9] Decades later, lamenting the junior high school's relative failure to meet these goals, Dr. William Alexander issued a call for a new "middle school" that would respond more explicitly to the academic and personal development of every young adolescent. He asserted that the goal of these schools should be *to stimulate in the child a love for learning, an attitude of inquiry, a passion for truth and beauty, a questioning mind. The learning of right answers is not enough...beyond answers alone, we must help children ask the right questions, and discover their answers through creative thinking, reasoning, judging, and understanding.*[10]

The 60 years since Alexander's landmark lecture have only heightened the urgency for schools to be responsive to the nature, needs, and identities of young adolescents. Alexander's belief that "the learning of right answers is not enough" is even more relevant in today's era of ready access to information than it was in 1963. Many school functions, such as teaching the tools of communication and inquiry, helping students acquire fundamental skills and knowledge, and promoting democratic citizenship, remain valid. Thriving now and in the future, however, demands more than a basic understanding of reading, writing, and mathematics. It requires students to learn how to learn, and to assess the veracity and merits of the vast amount of information available to them. Moreover, they need the ability to solve complex interdisciplinary problems, both individually and in collaboration with others.

In this publication, we offer a set of attributes and characteristics that define successful middle schools. These descriptors, rooted in research and experience, provide a framework for creating the learning environments and opportunities that all young adolescents deserve. One profound lesson learned in more than 60 years of active middle school practice, research, and advocacy is that these attributes and characteristics are interdependent and need to be implemented in concert.[11] While it can be tempting to selectively adopt those characteristics that appear to be achievable or more appropriate for a school or particular situation, each characteristic is part of a larger whole. Successful schools for young adolescents implement the full range of structures, supports, and practices known to be most effective with this age group. It is essential to recognize that the areas of development, including physical, intellectual, moral, psychological, and social-emotional, and various social identities such as race, ethnicity, social class, gender, sexual orientation, religion, and exceptionality, are inexorably intertwined. The achievement of academic success is highly dependent on other developmental and identity needs also being met.

A second enduring lesson from the past six decades is the recognition that young adolescents need, deserve, and benefit from middle grades practices regardless of a school's grade configuration. Young adolescents are not only educated in middle schools, they are taught in a range of settings including upper elementary, intermediate, junior high, and lower secondary schools. What matters most is not the particular grade span within the building but rather the quality of the learning opportunities students experience.[12] Middle schoolers benefit from an increasing focus on autonomy, belonging, competence, and identity,[13] regardless of the sign on their school walls or language on the school website. In this text, the term "middle school" refers to any school that serves young adolescents, including those learning environments that may be virtual.

We urge everyone involved in the lives of young adolescents to become familiar with the contents of this framework in order to advocate knowledgeably for successful middle schools. This call to action requires a recommitment to successful middle school practices by some and a newfound commitment by others. Educating young adolescents responsively and equitably requires the best from us all.

Educators can engage colleagues in discussion about this position paper, sharing views, clarifying thinking, and considering the implications of putting the concepts more fully into practice. Students can unpack the characteristics and consider how their experiences compare to those described. School leaders can partner with faculty to integrate it into their school's professional development. They can also engage relevant stakeholders—boards of education, district office personnel, and families— in learning experiences that will increase their knowledge and understanding of the academic, developmental, cultural and social needs of the young adolescents in their care. Together, a school community can assess the degree to which its school currently implements the features of a successful school and, subsequently, develop an improvement plan aimed at full implementation of the recommended characteristics.

If we all take these critical steps, we will build successful middle schools, schools that are responsive and equitable, in which all students can thrive.

The Successful Middle School
This We Believe

AMLE believes that the following five essential attributes of successful schools can be realized and achieved best through the 18 characteristics detailed on pages 11-53. To understand them better, these characteristics are grouped in three categories— Culture and Community; Curriculum, Instruction, and Assessment; and Leadership and Organization. The characteristics are, however, interdependent and need to be implemented in concert.

Essential Attributes

AMLE affirms that an education for young adolescents must be:

Responsive

Using the distinctive nature and identities of young adolescents as the foundation upon which all decisions about school are made.

Challenging

Cultivating high expectations and advancing learning for every member of the school community.

Empowering

Facilitating environments in which students take responsibility for their own learning and contribute positively to the world around them.

Equitable

Providing socially just learning opportunities and environments for every student.

Engaging

Fostering a learning atmosphere that is relevant, participatory, and motivating for all learners.

Get a printable PDF of the essential attributes and characteristics at amle.org/SMS

Characteristics

Successful middle schools exhibit the following 18 characteristics:

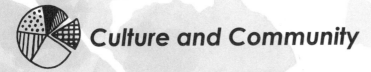

Culture and Community

— Educators respect and value young adolescents.

— The school environment is welcoming, inclusive, and affirming for all.

— Every student's academic and personal development is guided by an adult advocate.

— School safety is addressed proactively, justly, and thoughtfully.

— Comprehensive counseling and support services meet the needs of young adolescents.

— The school engages families as valued partners.

— The school collaborates with community and business partners.

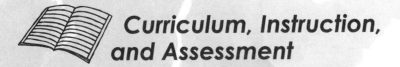

Curriculum, Instruction, and Assessment

— Educators are specifically prepared to teach young adolescents and possess a depth of understanding in the content areas they teach

— Curriculum is challenging, exploratory, integrative, and diverse.

— Health, wellness, and social-emotional competence are supported in curricula, school-wide programs, and related policies.

— Instruction fosters learning that is active, purposeful, and democratic

— Varied and ongoing assessments advance learning as well as measure it.

Leadership and Organization

— A shared vision developed by all stakeholders guides every decision.

— Policies and practices are student-centered, unbiased, and fairly implemented.

— Leaders are committed to and knowledgeable about young adolescents, equitable practices, and educational research.

— Leaders demonstrate courage and collaboration.

— Professional learning for all staff is relevant, long term, and job embedded.

— Organizational structures foster purposeful learning and meaningful relationships.

I Am...True

By Noah B., Grade 7

A magnet he gave me
That said TRUE
Like a sock and the shoe
My history teacher helped me the whole way through

Don't be delirious
Don't be too serious
He said to me
He said to you

Only be
TRUE
That Means
ONLY
THE
REAL
YOU
WILL
DO

That's what he expected of me
That's what he'll expect of you
Standing up is what he'll do for you
He will protect you
From those who hate you
Like he did for me
Teaching me to be FREE
From the people who were mean to me

He makes your brain ding with a zing
When he teaches you new things

He can be your friend and this is the end
Please do not forget If you haven't yet
To say thank you
To the teachers who are
Far and few
And are always
TRUE

It is those few
That are
The greatest and best

Culture and Community

Educators respect and value young adolescents.

Middle grades teachers' relationships with students have a profound impact on young adolescents' sense of belonging in school.[14] Positive student-teacher relationships are created when students feel valued, respected, cared for, encouraged, and listened to by their teachers.[15] Middle school students' sense of belonging is linked to many important outcomes, including increased engagement, motivation, academic achievement, positive attitudes toward school, and a decrease in absenteeism and at-risk behaviors.[16] Young adolescents voice that caring teachers value them both as learners and as individuals.[17]

Effective middle school educators engage in developmentally responsive practices that also respond to young adolescents' multiple identities. While age represents an important shared identity across middle schoolers, other social identities such as race, ethnicity, socio-economic status, sexual orientation, gender, dis/ability, and religion equally contribute to who young adolescents are and to their experiences in and outside of school.[18] Middle grades educators who value young adolescents acknowledge these multiple and intersecting identities and seek to cultivate relationships, design curriculum, and establish learning environments that support, affirm, and honor youth holistically.[19]

Middle grades educators enjoy being with young adolescents, think positively about them, and appreciate the dynamics of the ever-changing youth culture. They pay attention to and learn about the beliefs, values, and norms of their students. Not trivializing youth culture, middle grades educators examine young adolescents' participation in popular trends and their choices in language, music, and fashion to understand what youth are trying to convey through these and other forms of expressions.[20] They seek to understand aspects of students' digital worlds, such as social media and gaming. They then support, accept, and meet students where they are currently, while also encouraging their continuous identity development.[21]

Middle grades educators demonstrate that they value students by listening intensively to their students' words, observing their actions, and being attuned to their silences in order to actively respond to their needs.[22] These educators support students' social-emotional learning in school and in partnership with students' families. They recognize that students face many challenges that can be traumatic and therefore work collaboratively as educators to design schools that are spaces of healing for students.[23] In addition, they speak up for and stand by youth when social injustices that explicitly or implicitly impact them, their families, or communities occur.[24]

Such educators are inevitably role models for students. They realize their own behaviors send influential messages to young adolescents and so practice those qualities of heart and mind they want young adolescents to emulate. They model inclusive, democratic, anti-oppressive, and team-oriented approaches to teaching and learning. When such dedicated and knowledgeable middle grades educators work together, they create exciting and equitable learning experiences for all students. Their professional commitment and passion make a positive difference in the life of every young adolescent they teach.

The school environment is welcoming, inclusive, and affirming for all.

Middle school educators purposefully foster a culture that sustains the dignity of all members within the school community. This includes students, their families, local community members, and the staff who work within the school. Equal attention is also placed on cultivating individual classroom cultures that support the learning and development of young adolescent learners. Affirming classroom communities, whether physical or virtual, are formed when students' identities are valued and respected by their teachers

In their own words...

Sarina C., Grade 7

My favorite thing about middle school is the relationships you build with people, whether it be a kind teacher or a great group of friends.

and peers; students' experiences are honored; activities that students enjoy are incorporated into the curriculum; and social, emotional, and academic learning are supported.

As students transition into the middle grades, their social interactions with their peers increase and become more important and complex. Successful middle grades educators develop socially-accepting learning environments, knowing that peer relationships impact students' adjustment in school.[25] Students' sense of belonging is increased through peer emotional support, such as when students feel that their peers like and care about them, and peer academic support, such as when students are willing to help their peers answer questions or assist with homework.[26] Conversely, peer rejection, when students are actively disliked or excluded by their peers, can result in increased social anxiety, aggression, loneliness, and poor academic performance.[27] Even short instances of peer rejection impact students' well-being, and prolonged moments of peer rejection can have sustaining effects that last into adulthood.

To support positive peer relationships, teachers intentionally monitor peer hierarchies and interactions in classrooms and other common areas such as hallways, playgrounds, and school lunchrooms.[28] Teachers also foster cooperative-oriented classrooms that encourage collaboration versus competitive-oriented classrooms that can reinforce and contribute to social status rankings.[29] Regularly incorporating social and emotional learning skills such as empathy, civic-mindfulness, and relationship skills can help establish and maintain inclusive school environments. In addition, embedding designated times into the school day, such as morning meetings or advisory, where students can discuss their thoughts and express how they are feeling, can also serve to build community.

In their own words...
Nehemiah H., Grade 6

Over the past year, you have shown me what it's like to have people who truly care.

Middle grades educators acknowledge that prejudices such as racism, xenophobia, ableism, religious intolerance, sexism, homophobia, transphobia, and classism are present in schools and often are broadly labeled as bullying.[30] However, it is important for educators to explicitly recognize and name bigotry when it exists. This helps students to see when their actions or others are discriminatory and reflective of prejudice beliefs. In affirming and inclusive schools, positive behavioral and social expectations are clearly communicated and equitably applied and upheld. Prejudiced actions are directly addressed by enforcing anti-discrimination policies and developing a school-wide system in which students can safely report student victimization.[31]

An inclusive school climate is established through implementing intentional and thoughtful practices. For example, educators work to foster interethnic friendships as such relationships help to reduce racial prejudices and improve social, emotional, and cultural competencies.[32] "Safe space" posters, displayed throughout the school building let LGBTQ students know they are welcomed and will be supported. Furthermore, educators provide students with tools that support and encourage upstander behaviors as part of bullying and prejudice intervention education.[33] These actions create a school culture in which all members, including students, actively work together to sustain a welcoming school community.

To build affirming and inclusive middle schools requires educators to examine their own biases. Even the most well-intentioned educators have implicit biases that influence their teaching practices.[34] Implicit bias is a normal part of human cognitive functioning and is often connected to positive and negative stereotypes around various identities such as race, gender, and class. It is precisely because of educators' commitment to supporting their students that it is important for educators to be aware of how their implicit bias impacts their teaching in order to reduce unintended inequitable outcomes.[35]

Educators can examine both their explicit and implicit biases by asking difficult but important questions[36] such as *How do stereotypes shape the way I see students, families, and the local community? What assumptions guide my interactions with students, families, and the local community? How do my own experiences and privilege limit my understanding about students, families, and the local community?* Reflecting on these questions is especially important for teachers whose experiences and identities differ from their students. These and other questions about disciplinary practices, curricular choices, and family engagement directly relate to understanding and addressing bias. They therefore are embedded in middle grades teachers' ongoing practice and professional development. When coupled with conversations with students and families, such questions allow teachers to continuously examine if the school environment is welcoming and affirming of all students, instead of merely a subset.

Every student's academic and personal development is guided by an adult advocate.

Successful middle schools are intentionally designed to promote young adolescents' academic success and social-emotional growth. Advocating for students' overall well-being, then, is fundamental to the school's culture. Advocacy is not limited to a singular event or a particular time in the schedule. Rather, it is an attitude of caring that translates into actions, big and small, when adults respond to the needs of each young adolescent in their charge. Because meaningful relationships between young adolescents and adults can foster positive academic and social outcomes,[37] middle schools look both within and beyond school personnel for support. Vetted and trusted tutors, community leaders, retired teachers, academic and athletic coaches, local business partners, and after-school program educators can serve as role models, mentors, and advocates.

Each student has one adult in the school who assumes special responsibility for this advocacy, acting as advisor to support that student's academic and personal development.[38] The adult advisor meets regularly with a small group of students during the school day in what is often called Advisory, Teacher Advisory, or TA. The purpose of this time is to provide academic and social-emotional mentorship and support, to create a sense of belonging and community within the school, and to facilitate a small community of learners.[39] Effective advisors respect and enjoy working with young adolescents, are knowledgeable about the development of this age group, and understand the various social identities that may influence students' experiences and opportunities. Advisors are not counselors, but they listen to and guide youth through the ups and downs of school life. They also know how and when to connect students with additional resources that might be beneficial. Such advisory efforts augment but do not replace comprehensive counseling and guidance services.

The advisor is the primary liaison between school and family, initiating contact with parents or guardians to seek and offer helpful information about the student's program and progress. Effective advisors reach out regularly to parents and caregivers to share stories of growth and other positive news about students. Advisors are in a position to recognize noteworthy changes in students, and families are key partners in helping educators understand students in a holistic way. Collaborating with families is an important task, particularly during early adolescence. It is not unusual for students seeking greater independence to prefer to keep home and school separate, but appropriate communication between home and school can be an important link to higher student achievement.[40] Successful middle schools ensure that educators receive ongoing professional development to help them fulfill this broad-based advocacy role.

Thoughtful scheduling and grouping strategies help advance this advocacy by enabling educators and students to build healthy relationships. The schedule reflects regular meetings of advisors and advisees, extended homerooms, advisory programs, or team-based mentorships, among other structures. During these times, students engage in developing social-emotional competence; compassion and empathy; a sense of belonging and affiliation; and the skills of collaboration, decision making, and goal setting. Successful middle schools provide continuity of advocacy, caring, and support that extends not only throughout the school day but throughout a student's entire middle grades experience.

In their own words...
Ankit M., Grade 6

There are some amazing things in middle school, but the best thing is the freedom and the privacy we get as we move about our day.

School safety is addressed proactively, justly, and thoughtfully.

School safety is first and foremost rooted in school climate. A safe, just, and inclusive climate provides the foundation for a responsive middle school. Knowing that physical and psychological safety is a necessary condition for learning,[41] middle school educators create this climate in many ways. They collaborate with students to develop proactive and positively stated expectations for their learning community. They help students develop social-emotional competence. And they teach students how to resolve conflicts constructively. Middle grades teachers understand that unsafe schools can cause trauma. They reflect on how their own words and actions affect students and carefully examine how potential biases might negatively affect students' feelings of safety. Overall, successful middle schools connect students meaningfully to teachers, peers, and the school to promote a strong sense of belonging for all learners.[42]

In successful middle schools, all policies and practices related to safety and climate reflect a deep commitment to justice. Such schools recognize that harsh discipline protocols and zero tolerance policies contribute to the school-to-prison pipeline, disproportionately affecting students of color, students from lower income backgrounds, students with learning disabilities, and students who identify as LGBTQ.[43] School staff members reject overly punitive policies that exclude youth from their educational rights; instead they adopt practices that are inclusive and promote restorative justice.[44] Such approaches focus on healing relationships and repairing harm when acts of misbehavior occur.[45]

In their own words...

Luis Pedro C., Grade 9

Middle school allows us to gain incredible experiences while we're young, it gives us confidence that we can do anything we want to.

A safe and healthy climate is also visible in the physical aspects of a school environment. Leaders understand that the use of metal detectors and school resource officers can reduce students' feelings of safety and ensure that their presence does not increase the occurrence of exclusionary practices.[46] The provision of safe and clean facilities conveys a clear message to students that the adults in their lives care about them and their learning. Responsive middle schools encourage student ownership of these spaces by inviting learners to create murals, cultivate community gardens, and otherwise contribute to the beautification of their shared environment in ways that make sense for their context.

Access to a physically and emotionally safe school is important for all students and particularly for students who have experienced trauma. A sense of safety depends heavily on positive connections and feelings of affiliation. Because trauma can undermine trust, educators in responsive schools spend time building positive relationships with students, understanding their behaviors, and responding in ways that help students feel safe and valued.[47]

Comprehensive counseling and support services meet the needs of young adolescents.

Young adolescents face innumerable choices—some of them risky—as well as many life circumstances beyond their control. Successful middle grades schools provide specialized professionals who are readily available to assist students in negotiating their lives both in and out of school. Counselors, school psychologists, social workers, school nurses, cultural and linguistic interpreters, community liaisons, and others help youth with possible learning challenges, social adjustments, homelife issues, and health problems.

In concert with teachers and administrators, these professionals use their knowledge and skills to promote students' academic progress and personal well-being. Consistent interaction among specialists, teachers, and families helps to assure that student behaviors are accurately and justly assessed, and learning needs are met. All staff members are aware of the appropriate referral services and procedures to recommend students for specialized services.

As professionally prepared specialists, school counselors spend most of their time working directly with students and faculty rather than on administrative tasks. They coordinate support services to articulate and align them with those of the district's elementary and high schools. They also collaborate to access and coordinate community-based services to address a range of issues, such as when students experience housing or food insecurity.

School counselors are well positioned to support teachers in advisory programs, model and facilitate activities, and offer one-on-one and small-group sessions for students as needed. They share their expertise with teams and individual teachers, sponsor constructive conflict resolution and peer mediation programs, and support restorative practices. Counselors also meet with families, often in conjunction with an advisor, individual teacher, or team.

In addition, counselors play a key role in establishing environments where all students feel safe and included. They place special emphasis on marginalized populations, knowing that alliances and affinity groups can help to foster a positive, protective, and inclusive environment. For example, LGBTQ students have higher rates of depression, more suicide attempts, and lower self-esteem than their peers.[48] In schools with Gay-Straight Alliances, both youth in general and LGBTQ students in particular report less victimization and greater overall well-being.[49] Similarly, because early adolescence is a critical phase for forming ethnic-racial identity,[50] counselors actively support the promotion of middle schoolers' cultural assets.[51]

School counselors facilitate multidimensional transition programs as students enter and exit the middle grades. Many students feel anxious about transitioning to the middle grades and interventions that help students understand these feelings as common and temporary can positively affect their achievement, behavior, and well-being.[52] Such programs help students gain confidence in managing the transition and engage families in exploring how various middle grades course options may affect high school programming. Identifying the needs of each student and mapping out transition programs with appropriate stakeholders, including student input and engagement, are essential components of effective transition planning.[53]

The school engages families as valued partners.

Schools do not educate young adolescents alone, as students' families play an important role in their education. Middle grades educators are mindful that students' family dynamics vary with some students living with extended family members, foster parents, and in shared custody situations. Regardless of a student's family dynamics, research clearly links the involvement of families with higher levels of student achievement, improved student behavior, increased school attendance, improved student emotional well-being, and greater overall support for schools.[54] Hence, middle schools that partner with families provide the best possible learning experiences for young adolescents.

Standards promoting home-school partnerships are essential and should be used in every middle school. However, family involvement in the middle grades is not without challenge as family engagement often decreases as students transition from elementary school to middle school.[55] Caregivers of young adolescents are often uncertain about how they can be involved in this new, and often larger, school and may also be unsure about the most appropriate way to deal with their rapidly changing and maturing child.[56] Regardless of these uncertainties, families want their children to be successful in and out of school and they provide great insight into what works best for their children academically and socio-emotionally. When middle school educators purposefully engage families in ways that respect their dignity, acknowledge and value their expertise, and invite their contributions to schools, they forge positive home-school bonds.[57]

Research indicates that most caregivers are involved in their child's education, including those often labeled by educators as disengaged.[58] Relying on traditional views of family involvement, such as volunteering or participating in parent-teacher conferences, more often than not negatively positions families of color and families who are economically disadvantaged as disengaged.[59] It is important to consider how factors such as family norms, composition, cultural backgrounds, language, and socio-economic status can impact how families are involved in their child's education.[60] How schools respond to these factors directly impacts how welcome families feel in schools and how they participate in school-based engagement activities.[61] Middle school educators develop these understandings by fostering regular two-way communication and authentically listening to the values, needs, and concerns of families.[62] They then use this information to collaboratively build opportunities for active family-school partnerships that support student learning.

Middle schools that foster multifaceted and bi-directional family engagement cultivate stronger family-school partnerships and increase opportunities for collaboration. Successful middle schools, therefore, promote family involvement by involving caregivers in decision making at school, sponsoring parent/guardian education programs, creating and maintaining links between home and school, initiating volunteer programs, establishing coordinated home-school learning experiences, and by being actively engaged in the local community.[63] Administrators and faculty members in these schools solicit input from families in a variety of ways: holding meetings in community centers; being visible in community-based events; using language interpreters; or setting up a family learning center where caregivers can obtain information, have materials translated,[64] and meet with school officials and other caregivers. School newsletters, progress report cards, parent-teacher conferences, e-mail, text messages, class websites, web-based parent portals, social media, and student-led conferences are a few of many valuable communication tools used to inform and involve caregivers and community members.

The school collaborates with community and business partners.

Genuine, innovative, and sustainable community partnerships are a fundamental component of successful schools for young adolescents. Therefore, middle schools seek appropriate partnerships with businesses, social service agencies, universities, non-profit organizations, and local municipalities with purposes consistent with the school's mission.[65] In

In their own words...
Ainsley B., Grade 8

Every day they teach me how to be a more honest person, have integrity, be productive, and how to simply act. That's what middle school teachers should be doing.

meaningful partnerships, both school and community resources and expertise are integrated to support student academic success, strengthen students' and families' overall well-being, and foster engaged communities.[66] Community partnerships can also advance the learning of middle grades educators, enabling them to develop a deeper cultural understanding of students' lives. Such a partnership increases collective accountability, which helps to facilitate systemic changes in schools and the communities in which students live. These partnerships are especially powerful resources for schools relying on virtual, distance, or remote learning strategies.

The community is a robust resource, serving as a site for authentic learning experiences that cannot be provided in a classroom, as a source of materials and guest experts, and providing assistance in appropriate learning initiatives for students and faculty. Middle school curriculum becomes relevant when learning is connected to real-life experiences. Therefore, successful middle schools integrate the community as curriculum and as a learning space where students become involved in apprenticeships, shadow studies, service-learning projects, and after-school programs.[67] The community is a key feature as educators implement place-based education and leverage the local environment as a primary source of learning.[68]

In true partnerships, all parties benefit, share mutually understood roles and expectations, and have an understanding of each other's organizational context and mission. Formal structures are created, such as memoranda of understanding between schools and community organizations to ensure agreements are reached.[69] Collaborative efforts are enhanced when community stakeholders are invited to serve on school committees and leadership teams. Similarly, school administrators and teachers can volunteer to serve on community task forces. Involving community stakeholders in schools and school members in communities creates a shared power dynamic in which both entities demonstrate their commitment, gain an appreciation of each other's context, and identify where resources and expertise align to support what's best for young adolescents in and out of schools.

School-community partnerships can be both local and global.[70] As middle school leaders build meaningful and needed relationships with stakeholders in the communities where their students live, the value of and ability to engage in broader partnerships should also be considered. Digital tools enable access to global partners, such as businesses and organizations that are not represented in a school's local community. Such partnerships can be extremely valuable for supporting students' cultural and global awareness and in expanding access to resources needed to advance student learning.

My Favorite Teachers

By Katherine T., Grade 7

Hair bounces on her shoulders
Her warm smile
creases her cheeks
paper cascades from every corner of the room
pencils
poke the air above me

He moves his hands gracefullythrough the cinnamon-apple air
Quotes litter the walls
and we can't resist but sing them
with a flick of his wrist
he gives his 'possums' candy
and we drown in Starbursts.

She's a whirlwind of energy
her scarf flying, electrifying
giggles fill the air.
Escape rooms, assembly lines
and more fill the room
and we enter with giddy excitement.

LEGOS and Star Wars galore
a clock that makes it hard to figure out the time
booming laughs abound
We're always on our feet
ready to catch the next mint
or homework pass

Bean bag chairs
a pepperminty smell
dim lights cast a soft glow through the room
soft words are shared
floating through the tranquil space

These teachers
shaped my brain
filled it with nuggets of knowledge
that cascade out of my mouth,
and for them I am forever grateful.

Curriculum, Instruction, and Assessment

Educators are specifically prepared to teach young adolescents and possess a depth of understanding in the content areas they teach.

Effective middle grades teachers and administrators are specifically prepared to work with and advocate for young adolescents through specialized middle grades professional preparation. This occurs prior to teaching young adolescents and then continues through ongoing professional development as they pursue their careers. Such educators are collaborators who know how to form learning partnerships with their students, implement culturally and linguistically sustaining practices,[71] and demonstrate empathy while engaging students in significant and relevant academic learning experiences. Specialized middle grades preparation helps educators appreciate the uniqueness of young adolescents, realize their intellectual capabilities, and utilize discipline knowledge in meaningful ways to support student learning, while increasing persistence and commitment to working with young adolescents.[72]

Essential elements of middle grades professional preparation programs include a deep understanding of young adolescents, their development, and their diverse identities; middle school philosophy and organization; knowledge of the content area(s) taught; middle school curriculum; middle grades planning, instruction, and assessment; and opportunities to demonstrate professional roles and ethical behaviors.[73] Preferably, middle grades professional preparation programs require proficiency in at least two content areas in order to support both in-depth disciplinary knowledge and meaningful curriculum integration.[74]

Middle grades professional preparation incorporates opportunities for preservice teachers to engage in early, continuous, and high-quality clinical experiences in middle grades classrooms. Collaborative and mutually beneficial partnerships between universities and schools provide preservice teachers an opportunity to make connections between theory and practice, foster the continuous development of practicing teachers, and collectively work to improve middle grades students' learning experiences.[75] Clinical experiences are enhanced when they include community-based experiences, allowing preservice teachers to develop their understanding of how to leverage local cultures and places to make learning relevant for their students.[76]

Successful middle grades professional preparation programs integrate equity-oriented and anti-racist pedagogies throughout preservice teachers' programs to prepare them to address issues of equity, diversity, and social justice in their future classrooms.[77] Preservice teachers also engage in ongoing critical reflection that challenges their assumptions, biases, and stereotypes, in order to help them unlearn deficit perspectives about historically disenfranchised and marginalized students, families, and communities.[78] Together clinical experiences and university courses prepare teachers to implement equitable practices in middle grades classrooms and moves teaching from good intentions to effective action,[79] thus developing their ability to become advocates for change.[80]

Though middle grades teacher preparation matters, there are many middle grades teachers and administrators whose pathways to the profession required limited or no specialized middle grades training.[81] Thus, it is imperative that middle grades educators are engaged in professional development that strengthens their ability to support student learning. Induction programs for beginning middle grades teachers help to prepare all educators, and especially those without specialized middle grades preparation, with the skills, knowledge, and dispositions that are distinctively needed to work with young adolescent learners.[82]

Young adolescents deserve educators who are prepared and deeply committed to working with them. State departments of education, professional practice boards, and institutions of higher learning share responsibility for developing appropriate programs to provide both initial preparation and graduate programs leading to specific middle grades teacher and administrator preparation and middle grades licensure. Although successful schools and school districts provide ongoing professional development, they complement those efforts with the resources offered by professional associations, state departments, colleges, and universities.

Curriculum is challenging, exploratory, integrative, and diverse.

A middle grades curriculum invites students to learn about matters of personal, social, moral, and ethical significance. It addresses external expectations, such as state-wide or district-adopted standards, while appealing to young adolescents and offering them opportunities to pose and answer questions that are important to them. The curriculum also introduces students to multiple, diverse perspectives and viewpoints. In other words, an effective middle grades curriculum must be challenging, exploratory, integrative, and diverse, from both the student's and the teacher's perspective.

Recognizing that covering the content and learning the content are not synonymous, and that having valuable academic standards does not demand a uniform, prescribed curriculum, middle grades teachers and other curriculum developers work diligently to provide meaningful educational experiences for young adolescents. A responsive middle school curriculum focuses on issues of social and personal consequence and involves complex tasks. It is often divided into units or projects that are organized around a theme, question, or mix of teachers' goals and students' questions rather than around separate subjects. Further, the curriculum encompasses not only the classes designed to advance specific skills and knowledge but also school-wide services and programs such as guidance, clubs and interest groups, music and drama productions, student government, service activities, and sports.

The "hidden curriculum"—what students learn indirectly but surely from the people with whom they interact, the structures in which they work, and the issues that inevitably occur[83]—has a powerful influence on students' education and lives. In fact, this aspect of learning is sometimes so profound and long-lasting that it overrides learning that is more explicit. Successful

In their own words...
Liza B., Grade 8

Middle school is such an important part of your life because you get to see what subjects you like before entering high school when you get to choose what subjects you take.

middle grades educators understand that issues related to racism, social justice, privilege, oppression, and civil rights are regularly omitted or under-emphasized in curriculum.[84] They critically examine materials to identify what is missing or misrepresented in order to provide a more inclusive and anti-racist curriculum, and facilitate explicit and developmentally appropriate conversations about race.[85] They also invite students to question curricular materials and examine whose voices are missing, remaining open to such critiques. Teachers in successful middle grades schools skillfully interweave the planned curriculum with the unplanned, ensuring each student feels valued and is treated equitably.

Challenging

Challenging curriculum addresses substantive concepts and skills and is appropriately geared to each student's level of understanding and readiness. Creating or adapting curriculum to challenge each student requires significant planning, flexibility, and collaboration among educators, families, and the students themselves. Attuned to the vast developmental and identity-related diversity of their learners, middle school teachers know students' prior experiences, social and cultural backgrounds, and learning preferences. This knowledge, along with thoughtful use of formative and summative assessment data, informs curriculum. In successful middle schools, learning tasks are perceived as achievable, even if difficult, and reflect high expectations for all students.

Because technology makes vast amounts of knowledge and information readily and instantly accessible, challenging middle grades curriculum is not about accumulating facts. Rather, it is about assessing the veracity of sources and skillfully selecting and applying knowledge to solve complex problems, particularly those that are meaningful to young adolescents. Students are more likely to persist through the difficulties of challenging curriculum when it is also personally meaningful and engaging.[86]

Expecting students to grapple with and master advanced concepts and skills requires middle grades teachers to stretch themselves well beyond "covering material." School administrators therefore ensure that teachers have sufficient time and support to both deepen their knowledge of content and pedagogy and design challenging learning opportunities. Using their professional judgment and in consultation with students, teachers guide the selection of ideas and concepts for in-depth study. To help these issues come alive, teachers invite students to examine values, assumptions, basic principles, and alternative points of view, addressing why things happen as well as how. Students learn skills and concepts in context as they become explorers, thinkers, and communicators.

Exploratory

The middle school is the finding place, a place that invites young adolescents to be adventuresome, curious explorers. Therefore, the general approach for the entire curriculum at this level is one of exploration. Although some experiences or courses may be labeled exploratory, it should not be assumed they are, therefore, nonacademic. Exploratory courses are an essential feature of a successful middle school. Similarly, a solid academic experience properly designed is exploratory. Exploration is an attitude and approach, not a classification of content.

Middle school is a time for students to explore and learn about themselves and the world around them. If youth pass through early adolescence without broad, exploratory experiences, their future lives may be needlessly restricted. They deserve chances to ascertain their special interests and aptitudes, to engage in activities that will broaden their views of the world and of themselves. This is particularly true for students who may not have access to such opportunities outside of school.

They need, for instance, the chance to conduct science experiments, though they may never choose to work in a lab; be a member of a musical group, though they may never choose to become a professional musician; to write in multiple formats, though they may never choose to publish professionally;

to have a part in a play, though never choose to become a paid actor; to play on a team, though never choose to become a career athlete; or to create visual images through drawing and painting, though never choose to become an artist. Curriculum that is exploratory has potential career value yet also leads to healthy recreational pursuits that enrich life and carry over into adulthood. Exploratory curriculum is a fundamental component of a school serving young adolescents.

Integrative

An integrative curriculum responds to the inquisitive nature of young adolescents by organizing curriculum around significant problems and issues in society.[87] It invites students to pursue answers to questions they have about themselves, their communities, and the world. Prescribed curriculum often focuses on finding answers to questions young adolescents never ask. In contrast, when they examine problems they have identified and take steps to solve them, students develop critical thinking, decision making, creativity, and other deeper learning outcomes.[88]

An integrative curriculum focuses both on inquiry and action.[89] This curricular approach helps students develop a deep understanding of academic knowledge; a critical awareness of the historical, social, and cultural context of society; and the proficiencies needed to enact change. Educators support students' understanding of local, national, and global civic responsibilities and co-facilitate opportunities for them to demonstrate active citizenship through participation in endeavors that benefit their schools and broader communities.[90] At the same time, students cultivate critical consciousness and the skill sets needed to be informed and active citizens in a democracy.

Because real-life issues are multifaceted and interdisciplinary, curriculum that is rooted in students' observations of their own lives can be integrative, relevant, and meaningful.[91] Middle school curriculum focuses not only on what students may need later in life; it integrates students' histories to help them see how they can use what they are learning in the here and now.[92] This learning is facilitated through thoughtfully designed interdisciplinary experiences, studies, and units that help students see the integrated nature of knowledge and the many connections that link various topics, concepts, and subjects.[93] Though curriculum integration can be guided by one teacher, learning is enhanced when curriculum is planned and implemented by an interdisciplinary team of educators. Multiliteracies[94] are advanced and practiced wherever they apply, rather than taught in isolation.

In successful middle schools, students make decisions about curricular goals and content, and explore curriculum through a range of modes, including apprenticeships, independent study, small group work, and special interest experiences. Making curriculum integrative and relevant, however, does not mean limiting topics and material to students' pre-existing interests. Successful middle schools also foster new interests and open doors to new knowledge and opportunities. Youth benefit from studying concepts and learning skills in areas that interest them as well as in those determined by adults. As young adolescents develop greater independence, they help make curriculum relevant by personalizing and taking increasing ownership of their education.

Diverse

Middle grades curriculum is most meaningful when it exposes students to multiple viewpoints and encourages young adolescents to explore diverse perspectives. It invites them to consider new ideas and to question old ones. Not only do young adolescents develop an increased awareness of diversity and, subsequently, stereotypes, they also have a heightened understanding of how power and privilege results in differences among groups of people.[95] Particularly, young adolescents reflect on and question how their own cultural and social identity groups relate to, differ from, and are in position to other groups.[96] If not addressed in school, students can form unchallenged views about their own worth and the worth of others. Responsive middle school educators acknowledge that students have these important and evolving thoughts around their exploration of identity.[97] They use curriculum constructively to help students answer questions in ways that are affirming while also supporting students' awareness of their own privileges, such as racial, social class, and cis-gender.[98]

Such a curriculum requires educators to design learning that builds on and sustains students' cultural and linguistic backgrounds and experiences.[99] Middle grades educators understand that a colorblind approach to teaching that does not acknowledge the race or ethnicity of students creates missed opportunities for educators to make curriculum relevant to students' lives.[100] Students need opportunities to see themselves and their multiple social identities reflected in the curriculum.[101] This encompasses traditional curricular components such as unit plans and instructional materials, as well as less-often considered aspects of the curriculum that frequently convey messages to students about who and what is valued in their school. These more subtle yet still visible components include the diversity found in displayed images in classrooms and school hallways; the diversity of the teaching staff and invited guest speakers; policies that regulate the ways that students' use their native languages within the classroom;[102] and topics of school-wide events, elective class offerings, and extracurricular activities.

Middle grades educators support students' understanding of their own identities while also developing their awareness of other existing cultures and perspectives. Curriculum that demonstrates an appreciation of diversity moves beyond a narrow focus of culture, such as food and clothing, that is intermittently incorporated in the curriculum through cultural celebration programs and fairs.[103] These aspects of multicultural education are valuable but insufficient because they still often center a Eurocentric curriculum where diversity is an add-on to a largely unchanged curriculum. Instead, students' cultural competencies are developed when culture is incorporated throughout the curriculum and includes complex discussions about various cultural beliefs, values, norms, histories, and experiences.

Students need sustained and fully integrated opportunities to learn diverse perspectives, learn in diverse ways, and learn how diverse people have contributed to the world across all subject disciplines. For example, students should read literature written from culturally diverse authors; discuss history using narratives from voices that are often excluded; learn about the scientific contributions of Black, Indigenous, and other people of color; and be taught mathematics in ways that account for how different cultures apply mathematics in their daily lives.[104] Such an approach allows students whose own cultures are often absent from curriculum to see themselves as creators and doers of mathematics, science, literacy, and other disciplines. It also simultaneously exposes all students to the vast diversity that exists in the world.

Middle grades students' social awareness is supported and learning becomes relevant when students use their subject matter knowledge and skills such as

literacy, mathematical reasoning, historical thinking, or scientific inquiry, to
deepen their understanding of important social issues.[105] Curriculum that
exposes students to diverse perspectives creates critical opportunities
for teachers to help students reexamine assumptions and stereotypes that
they may possess about their own or other social identity groups. Teachers
further students' understanding of multiple perspectives by cultivating the
skills needed to analyze bias found in media, peer and adult interactions,
and themselves.

Health, wellness, and social-emotional competence are supported in curricula, school-wide programs, and related policies.

Successful middle grades schools help students understand their own
development and equip them with the skills to cultivate healthy minds and
bodies. An emphasis on health, wellness, and social-emotional competence
permeates the curriculum and the school culture. School policies enable and
support this emphasis, and the school leverages home-school-community
partnerships to promote a healthy and safe learning environment.

A coordinated health and wellness program focuses on those areas of
students' personal lives that enhance or interfere with learning. The benefits
and attributes of healthy lifestyles are included in the curriculum and the
learning environment as a whole. Student-centered and developmentally
appropriate experiences address knowledge of the changing body and mind;
the risks associated with behaviors such as vaping, alcohol use, and drug
use; and the importance of healthy eating habits, including how to manage
the challenges of food insecurity and information about non-stigmatizing
breakfast and lunch offerings for students and families. Such programs

offer accurate information about healthy relationships, sexuality, and the importance of consent, given that middle school is a crucial time for youth to access critical health information and to understand sexual and gender identity development.[106]

Another important part of this comprehensive wellness program is regular physical education that improves students' cardiovascular fitness, coordination, agility, and strength. As their bodies and brains undergo dramatic changes, young adolescents benefit greatly from physical activity.[107] A responsive curriculum engages students in fulfilling health and fitness goals through personal wellness profiles, which are appropriate to individual students' development and identities. The school also emphasizes lifelong physical activities such as dance, martial arts, leisure sports, and fitness programs. Intramural and co-curricular activities that encourage physical activity are developmentally appropriate, open to all students, and comply with recognized standards. Schools that engage in interscholastic sports follow policies and practices that are developmentally and culturally appropriate for the young adolescents in their communities.

Successful middle schools also offer young adolescents a scheduled time for recess or other self-selected opportunities to engage in physical activity. Breaks and opportunities for movement are important wherever students may spend extended periods of time in sedentary positions, including both in-person and online learning settings. Even minor movement during recess can help counterbalance sedentary time at school, while also providing time for important social interactions.[108] Chances for self-selected movement can be built into exploratory programs, mid-morning breaks, lunchtime intramural activities, and clubs.[109]

Finally, social-emotional learning is a crucial component of a middle grades curriculum. Social-emotional competence can protect students from the adverse effects of mental health difficulties[110] and a lack of such competence is regularly linked to an increased chance of poor health, unemployment, and imprisonment.[111] A responsive middle grades school, therefore, offers students regular, integrated, and culturally sensitive opportunities to develop skills and adopt mindsets that will help them succeed in school and life. These include self- and social-awareness, self-management, relationship skills, and responsible decision-making. Students explore how to identify and manage their feelings, understand and empathize with others' points of view, communicate and connect with a range of people in a healthy way, and make positive choices.[112]

Instruction fosters learning that is active, purposeful, and democratic.

The distinctive characteristics of young adolescents provide the foundation for selecting learning and teaching strategies, just as they do for designing curriculum. Educators in successful middle schools use a wide variety of approaches to meet the needs of diverse learners. Their instruction leverages the skills, abilities, and prior knowledge of young adolescents.[113] When educators use asset-based pedagogies, where learning experiences capitalize on students' cultural, experiential, and personal backgrounds, new concepts build on the knowledge students already possess and make learning more relevant for them.[114] At the same time, middle grades teachers are sensitive to students' personal histories, especially traumatic events that can adversely impact student development. They integrate trauma-informed practices that mitigate in and out of school stressors and triggers that can hinder student learning.[115]

Instruction in successful middle schools fosters learning that is active, purposeful, and democratic. Students engage in learning situations that foster critical and creative thinking and acquire various ways of posing and answering questions. Teachers vary their instructional approaches often, eliciting curiosity, engaging students in purposeful learning, and offering opportunities for regular physical movement. Students in learning situations that offer autonomy show greater enjoyment of learning, increased persistence in academic work, and stronger academic performance.[116] Therefore, teachers use democratic approaches to instruction that involve students regularly in shared decision making and increase student responsibility. Ultimately, middle grades teachers consider students' needs, backgrounds, and the nature of the learning goal when choosing instructional approaches.[117]

Active

Successful middle schools are characterized by the active engagement of students. Young adolescents, and their teachers alike, often observe the importance of active, hands-on tasks in the middle grades.[118] Experiential approaches, such as project-based learning and service learning, are rooted in active learning. They typically emphasize *doing* over more passive modes of learning, immersing students in inquiry and investigation. During periods of sustained investigation, young adolescents pose meaningful questions, find resources, organize information into useful and meaningful constructs, and grasp long-term cause and effect relationships. By placing students in the driver's seat, these approaches respond to young adolescents' need for increased autonomy and can positively influence student engagement and achievement.[119]

Teachers of various specialties and subject areas collaborate to design active learning tasks that ensure appropriate challenges for all students. They use flexible and varied forms of group work to increase student engagement and achievement, with students being clustered randomly, or through intentional heterogeneous and homogeneous grouping. Collaborative work creates opportunities for students to become experts and share their expertise with their peers, which allows students to relate and learn from each other.[120]

Active learning can also be promoted through thoughtful technology integration. Young adolescents are large users of digital technologies.[121] Successful middle grades teachers understand that technology is much more than merely a screen for media consumption. Instead teachers focus on how digital technology can be used in service of active learning, enabling young adolescents to compose, create, construct, design, and invent.[122] Successful middle schools move beyond simply concentrating on the ratio of technology in the classroom, e.g. 1:1 computing, to using digital tools to increase academic outcomes, as well as student connectivity, motivation, and engagement.[123] Understanding and using digital tools also helps students develop personal responsibility and independence and prepares them for a digital world.[124] Students investigate the ramifications of living in a technological society by developing digital literacies and becoming fully informed and wise consumers of media. Additionally, successful middle schools ensure all students have equitable access to technology. While there is value in technology integration, inequities inherent in technology-based teaching and learning, such as access, do exist.[125] As with all teaching and instructional approaches, effective educators are mindful that approaches that might engage some students can at the same time

A Dance to Remember by Sarina C., Grade 7

I am in the play Beauty and the Beast *and I have a dance teacher who just is really sweet. When I thought of her once, I had an inspiration to draw a ballerina. She tells us to practice a lot, so I tried hard. I failed multiple times but eventually got it. It took a little while, but it was worth it. It makes me realize that even when a challenge seems difficult, we should never give up; and when we are done, it may feel like even more of an accomplishment than we thought.*

potentially disenfranchise other students. Due to the rapidly changing nature of technology, all educators engage in ongoing professional development to effectively integrate technology throughout teaching and learning.

Purposeful

Like many adults, middle schoolers appreciate doing work that matters. Successful middle schools, therefore, are designed to help them acquire this crucial sense of purpose. Youth engaged in purposeful activities experience higher self-esteem, achievement, and a sense of meaning in life.[126] Early adolescence is a time of considerable moral development, and issues of equity, injustice, and sustainability are important fodder for middle school curriculum. Students benefit from seeing that their work can make a difference in the world around them, which is why service learning is such a strong fit in middle school.[127] Service learning is often based on a challenging question or problem, which provides an authentic purpose for the learning. It offers students a chance to make decisions, take action, and see the results of their purposeful work. Students can develop a sense of agency and confidence in their ability to make change. Apprenticeships, design thinking, and maker-centered learning are just a few of the many additional formats that offer the potential for active and purposeful learning.

Purposeful learning, in its various forms, fosters the kind of deeper learning outcomes that are critical to later life success. Youth and adults alike can imagine the applicability of effective communication, problem solving, self-directed learning, innovation, and collaboration, the types of skills that have been referred to as 21st century skills, the 4 C's, and transferable skills, among other terms. As young adolescents develop greater capacity for adaptability and flexibility, they are increasingly able to build these kinds of skills.[128] Whatever the name, these skills are at the core of purposeful and deeper learning. Schools that offer deeper learning experiences to all students, including students of color and those with lower income backgrounds, have stronger academic outcomes, better attendance, and lower dropout rates.[129]

Democratic

During early adolescence, most students are developing the ability to imagine the future and think ahead. They begin to make decisions based less on impulse and more on goals.[130] And they benefit from opportunities to practice these skills. Middle school, therefore, is an ideal time to increase students' autonomy in and out of the classroom. Engaging students in planning and pursuing their own learning is a powerful and developmentally responsive way to increase autonomy. In successful middle schools, students have ongoing and meaningful input into what and how they learn.

To help young adolescents assume increased responsibility for their education, successful middle school teachers craft opportunities for students to develop greater self-awareness of their identities, needs, interests, and preferences. They invite students to use that self-knowledge to make choices about their learning. Since young adolescents learn best when they are engaged and motivated, students dialogue with teachers and one another about what and how to learn.[131] While offering student choice can be a first step toward establishing greater student autonomy, increasing students' input into what and how they learn means more than offering options. It means inviting students to ask, pursue, and answer questions of personal and social significance as part of the curriculum.[132]

Fortunately, there are many ways to design for student input and involvement. Goal-setting, passion projects, genius hours, and "hands-joined" activities—ones that teachers and students develop together—can serve as powerful entry points into involving students in decisions about their learning. Negotiated curriculum,[133] youth-adult partnership,[134] personalized learning,[135] and youth participatory action research[136] also offer well-established frameworks for engaging students meaningfully in their learning and in the world around them. Along the way, teachers provide intentional scaffolding, offer formative feedback, and curate useful resources.[137] Digital tools open up new instructional and learning opportunities that promote deeper learning and further democratize both content and the learning process. By inviting students into this powerful work, teachers are better able to personalize learning opportunities, open new and flexible pathways for learning, and assess in more authentic ways.[138]

Varied and ongoing assessments advance learning as well as measure it.

Learning in middle schools can be complex, messy, and wonderful, as students regularly set personal goals, chart their growth, work independently and collaboratively, and reflect on their progress. The wide variety of teaching approaches, the personalization of learning opportunities, and the presence of integrative curriculum call for assessment practices that are equally varied. Evidence of middle grades learning can be demonstrated in many ways, including presentations, performances, portfolios, projects, journals, artwork, teacher and peer feedback, teacher-designed tests, and audio or video documentation. While diverse, effective assessment practices are based on several common principles.

First, the purpose of assessment is to advance learning. Assessment serves a distinctly different function than evaluation. Evaluation uses data to place a value or judgement on the learning; assessment guides learning by describing a student's progress toward an objective.[139] Together, evaluation and assessment provide evidence for varied audiences that teaching and learning are progressing. While evaluation often serves broader school, district, or state-wide purposes, it is assessment that provides the most useful information to teachers, learners, families, and caregivers.

Second, effective assessment is fair and unbiased. Middle grades educators understand that cultural, linguistic, and social norms affect how learners understand, interpret, and respond to questions and prompts. They use assessment strategies that are appropriate for the student audience, contain no cultural biases, and provide feedback on students' actual skills and knowledge. Fair and unbiased assessment tools rely on contexts and words that are equally familiar to all students.

Third, assessment is a learning opportunity for students. Therefore, standards are clear from the outset, and assessment criteria are discussed and crafted in advance. Successful middle grades teachers plan with the end in mind, integrating learning scales, learning targets, rubrics, examples, benchmarks, and other tools to convey expectations in clear and coherent terminology. Because young adolescents benefit from actively assessing and judging their accomplishments, they can help identify these criteria, design assessment tools, and apply them to their own work. Doing so promotes students' understanding of quality and helps them internalize such standards. Self-assessment enables them to reflect on personal growth and learning and to communicate what they have learned. Students also identify further learning goals based on the teacher's descriptive feedback about the quality of their current work, which is provided in relation to the standard rather than comparison with other students. This ongoing feedback also outlines the necessary steps for further improvement in language that references the familiar assessment criteria.

Fourth, assessment is a learning opportunity for teachers. Rather than equating assessment with a test or a grade, effective middle grades teachers understand that good assessment provides them with essential information for keeping students on the path to academic success. They understand that young adolescents do not reach a uniform standard at the same time[140] and therefore enable students to work at their own pace. By using regular and ongoing formative assessment strategies, teachers obtain the necessary information about each of their students and adjust their instruction and curriculum accordingly. They learn what content they might need to re-teach, who might need to learn through a different modality, and which skills might need reinforcement. In doing so, they help students discover and understand their strengths and areas for growth.

Fifth, assessment is a learning opportunity for families and caregivers. Successful schools engage families in assessing and celebrating student work in many ways. Because middle schools regularly integrate project-based and service learning, students often share some form of presentation, performance, demonstration, or product with families and communities. Similarly, student-led conferences, when rooted in meaningful learning opportunities documented with self-assessed evidence, are especially valuable in helping adults understand students' growth and capabilities. Preparing for such conferences helps students discover and understand their own strengths, weaknesses, interests, and aptitudes. Overall, this communication between students, families, and teachers keeps home and school working together.

Finally, assessment fosters deeper learning outcomes, such as thinking critically and solving complex problems; incorporating feedback; collaborating and communicating effectively; and developing the academic mindsets necessary for self-direction and comprehension of academic content. Successful middle grades teachers prioritize these deeper learning outcomes and regularly rely on performances, portfolios, and projects to assess them.[141] They use competency-based, proficiency-based, or standards-based assessment practices to provide students with repeated opportunities to demonstrate their learning in authentic ways and well in advance of a summative assessment or evaluation.[142]

The Reunion *by AnLan X., Grade 7*

At my school, we do things as a team, whether it's finishing a project or thriving through a pandemic. The vibrant background represents our joyful atmosphere at school where everyone is encouraged to achieve their goal. The abstract body of people represents the school community all coming together to achieve a common goal which is represented by the red heart in the center of the painting. This painting shows that no matter where a person is in real life, they will always have a community that has their back.

My Locker

By Eliza L., Grade 7

It was my first memory
Of middle school.
It was an interesting memory
Of middle school.
That blue locker and I
Had quite a connection
Though forced.
This may seem hard to believe.
To startlingly despise the device that
Brings you freedom and security.
But this one did not.
Ask yourself if you would
Appreciate a locker
Smaller in size than most
With lots of scratches.
And so it doesn't look desirable.
And so it will always be.
It is broken.
Its small blue frame pops out any time
I or somebody else in my row closes their locker.
And so it always looks open.
And so it will always be.
It is conveniently located by the teacher lunchroom
Right by the corner.
And so constantly
I am almost run over.
And so it will always be.
But what can I do?
Nothing.
I had it fixed before the start of school
Ready to start with a fresh new locker
Instead finding a locker that broke once again.
I have come to accept it.
I tolerate it and it tolerates me.
It does a good enough job
Of not spilling all of my things.
And I do a good enough job
Of keeping it somewhat clean.
And so we do a good enough job
Of being frenemies.
And so I will let it be.
Because it will always be.

Leadership and Organization

A shared vision developed by all stakeholders guides every decision.

Vision is an acute sense of the possible. A successful middle school's vision lights the way toward achieving a responsive and equitable education for every young adolescent. It reveals how research and practice can work in harmony to create a school in which every student feels valued and experiences success. Effective leaders embrace the diversity of their communities and work collaboratively with a broad range of stakeholders to build this ambitious vision. The vision becomes the basis for a concise mission statement that is collaboratively developed and supported by students, families, educators, administrators, board of education members, and the community.

A successful middle school's vision and mission are based upon fundamental building blocks: the development and varied identities of young adolescents; policies and practices that ensure an equitable and just education for all; and research on effective teaching and learning. The vision and mission also take into account the district's educational philosophy, goals, and guidelines.

Because they are used to inform decisions about educational practice and policy, the vision and mission statements are reviewed and revised as circumstances change and new research and practices emerge. School leaders regularly ask for input into the statements from staff, students, families, and community members so that both serve as living statements that guide all decisions made about the school.

Policies and practices are student-centered, unbiased, and fairly implemented.

Middle schools' policies and practices significantly impact school culture, programming, instruction, improvement efforts, and family and community engagement. Successful middle grades educators and leaders intentionally examine the policies and practices that guide teaching and learning within their schools to ensure that all students' academic and personal needs are met. This goal is upheld when policies and practices are student-centered, anti-racist, academically rigorous, and responsive to the realities of students and their families' lives.

Middle school professionals are keenly aware of the historic and present inequitable education experiences and outcomes for students, particularly culturally and linguistically diverse, economically disadvantaged, and LGBTQ students. This is seen through disciplinary practices that result in higher school suspensions and expulsions rates of Black and LGBTQ students; school tracking practices that result in an overwhelming absence of Black, Indigenous, and Latinx students in gifted education; and underfunding of schools in impoverished communities.[143]

However, effective middle schools purposefully work to create equitable outcomes for students and their families. Such practices include incorporating service learning within the curriculum that connects learning to active community engagement, implementing clubs that demonstrate to students that their various identities are valued and welcomed, incorporating ethnic studies as an integrated part of the curriculum, using restorative justice approaches as an alternative to exclusionary and punitive discipline practices, and offering weekend and summer food programs to ensure that students who are food insecure have access to food when school is not in session.[144] Middle schools that implement such practices support the well-being and academic success of students while also showing their commitment to the communities in which they are located.

Engaging in schoolwide self-reflection is an essential component to ensure policies and practices are unbiased and reflect a commitment to diversity and inclusion. Just as individual educators must critically reflect on their own assumptions that guide their instruction and interactions with students, it is necessary to engage in critical reflection on school-wide structures, processes, and outcomes.[145] This includes examining textbook adoption and curriculum implementation for inclusivity of diverse perspectives, focusing on hiring practices to support the recruitment and retention of racially diverse middle grades educators,[146] and ensuring that the composition of school leadership teams that often make important decisions about the vision and mission of the school is representative of diverse voices and comprised of school administrators, staff, students, families, and community members.

Critical reflection about policies and practices is enhanced when coupled with school data collection that examines academic achievement, school climate, and disciplinary records. School-wide data supports administrators' holistic understanding of a school's performance, while analysis of disaggregated data by student demographics such as gender, students with free and reduced lunch, dis/ability, and ethnicity can help to illuminate disparities in academic outcomes and students' sense of belonging.[147] Systematically using various types of data to inform educator professional development and school improvement plans supports ongoing accountability and transformative education.

Leaders are committed to and knowledgeable about young adolescents, equitable practices, and educational research.

Effective leadership is critical to a school's success. Successful middle school leaders—whether administrators, teachers, or other staff members—possess a deep understanding of the middle schoolers with whom they work and the society in which they live.[148] These leaders are knowledgeable about early adolescence. They understand the varied identities youth possess, how those identities intersect, and how those identities may influence students' experiences and opportunities. And they apply this knowledge to create middle grades programs that advance students' learning and growth.

The middle school principal holds responsibility for ensuring that existing policies and practices make the school an equitable, just, and welcoming place. The principal models and drives a commitment to promoting equity, building an inclusive and anti-racist environment, and reducing disparities for people who may be systematically disadvantaged. Successful principals create regular and sustained opportunities for staff to engage in critical conversations focused on self-reflection and bias as one way to work toward these goals.

Effective leaders also consistently update their knowledge of educational research and use that research to inform school policies and practices. They understand how to leverage interdisciplinary teaming, flexible scheduling, and varied grouping strategies to build young adolescents' sense of belonging and competence. They promote curriculum, pedagogy, and assessment practices that foster middle schoolers' sense of agency, efficacy, and identity. They conduct audits to assess equity and inclusion in relation to school practices and policies. And they use this information to educate and empower others to make the necessary, often hard decisions, as a school addresses the education and well-being of each and every student.

A deep and unwavering commitment to the well-being of all young adolescents characterizes the successful middle grades principal. These exemplary leaders understand that they positively influence student achievement by fostering a safe and supportive learning climate, one characterized by high, consistent, and clear expectations for all students.[149] To build support for long-term, continuous school improvement, they educate colleagues, parents, policymakers, and community members about early adolescence, equitable practices, and relevant educational research.

Leaders demonstrate courage and collaboration.

As architects for change, courageous, collaborative leaders make a difference by putting their knowledge and beliefs into action. Their commitment to the successful education of every young adolescent helps them to confront inequitable, unjust, or developmentally inappropriate situations and to change practices that do not serve students' best interests.

While successful principals recognize and capitalize on their own strengths, they also engage the expertise of others. They assemble and work closely with a leadership team that includes teachers and other school professionals. They build a culture of collaboration that cultivates leadership skills in others, empowering others to make decisions and enact changes. They also value input from all members of the school community, intentionally seeking out the perspectives of educators, students, family and community members from historically marginalized groups.

Successful principals also understand that improving schools is a long-term proposition. To endure, new structures, programs, and practices require time and ongoing refinement to become integral to the school culture. Schools committed to the long-term implementation of effective practices must be collaborative enterprises. Therefore, effective principals create a strong climate by supporting teacher leadership of school-wide goals.[150] Knowing that collective teacher efficacy is a powerful lever for student achievement,[151] they build consistent opportunities for teachers to develop and collaborate toward those common goals. Overall, by skillfully supporting shared leadership, principals advance the leadership capacity in the school and ensure staff members have collective ownership of the school's direction.[152]

Professional learning for all staff is relevant, long term, and job embedded.

Successful middle grades educators continually aspire to improve and are committed to ongoing professional learning. They recognize the positive impact of their own learning on their students' academic growth and personal development.

Middle grades teacher professional development responds to the needs of adult learners. Like students, teachers possess varying identities, learning preferences, and levels of readiness. Effective professional development is customized and personalized to take these different needs into account. It incorporates active learning, integrates models of effective practice, and supports collaboration between and among educators. It is job-embedded, extends over a sustained duration, and is built on a model of ongoing coaching, feedback, and reflection.[153]

Well-designed professional development balances this personalization for individual educators with coherence for the school as a whole. Effective middle school leaders carefully craft a coherent school change agenda, focusing on what matters most and protecting educators from all-too-common initiative fatigue.[154] They facilitate and model learning, listen thoughtfully, and build a school culture that supports faculty to engage in reflective practice.

Whether individual or school-wide, effective middle grades professional development takes many forms, and school leaders play a key role in organizing and supporting these initiatives. Teachers establish professional learning communities to discuss shared readings, student data and work, and instructional and assessment strategies with one another. They lead and participate in multiple-phased workshops or programs focusing on school improvement practices or content knowledge. They reflect on how their identities may differ from those of their students and engage in critical conversations about bias and racism. They visit other schools, mentor novice teachers, learn from families and community members, engage with their students in participatory action research, attend conferences, and take university courses. Online opportunities further broaden teachers' professional networks while helping them to stay current with the latest research on teaching, learning, and young adolescents. The key to all learning opportunities is a deep focus on the improvement of education for young adolescents.

Organizational structures foster purposeful learning and meaningful relationships.

Successful middle schools intentionally organize people, time, and space to maximize young adolescents' growth and development. Large schools are often subdivided into "houses" or "schools-within-a-school" to further achieve a desired sense of connectedness. These subdivisions replicate on a smaller scale the same mix of grade levels and demographics that make up the school community as a whole. Such arrangements foster the long-term student-teacher relationships known to have educational and developmental value during these transition years.

In their own words...
Olivia P., Grade 8

...if we need help we help each other.

A signature component of middle schooling is the interdisciplinary team of two or more teachers working with a common group of students for a shared block of time, ideally in a proximate space. Effective teams serve as the foundation for a strong learning community. They offer youth opportunities to participate in team governance and explore democracy in action. They can provide young adolescents with a sense of belonging, social bonding, and connectedness.[155] They also can lead to improved student achievement, improved family engagement, and other positive outcomes.[156] Smaller teams of two or three teachers can be particularly effective in achieving these benefits, as they offer the potential for creativity, collaboration, and connectedness without the added complexity of more team members.[157] Teaming also offers positive outcomes for teachers' professional lives, with the potential to expand collegiality, bolster support, and enhance professional growth.[158] Keeping a team of teachers and students together for two or three years, as in looping and multiage teams, provides particular opportunities for teachers to establish sustained relationships with students and families.

To achieve these benefits, teaching teams require daily common planning time. Educators need regular opportunities to discuss how—and how well--they are meeting learners' needs. During common planning time, teachers plan how they will integrate curriculum and personalize learning. They analyze and reflect on assessment data and student work, discuss current research, and reflect on their team's effectiveness.[159] Addressing the concerns of individual students and day-to-day management details are also important topics on a team's agenda but these are balanced with the fundamental work of considering curriculum, instruction, and assessment. Often, teams appoint a leader to represent them on a school-wide leadership group that sets direction, provides feedback, and advances school improvement efforts. Whether organized formally or not, teachers of a particular subject also require opportunities to meet.

Creativity Flow by Hannah B., Grade 8

My inspiration for my artwork is how creative the students at my school can be. I was thinking about how just one student can have all these amazing unique ideas and I wanted to express it.

A responsive middle school schedule enables young adolescents to immerse deeply in meaningful learning experiences. Project-based learning, service learning, expeditionary learning, community-based learning, inquiry-based learning, and other experiential approaches are more powerfully enacted when teams have access to large and flexible amounts of time. A flexible block schedule—one over which the teaching teams themselves have control—enables the kind of active and meaningful learning opportunities that are appropriate for young adolescents. Flexible schedules enable educators to bring to life the challenging, integrative, relevant, and exploratory curriculum that middle schoolers deserve.

Effective schedules also support the flexible grouping of students. Academic tracking results in many negative effects, including decreases in student motivation and self-esteem, unequal learning opportunities, and declines in the overall quality of education. These negative outcomes disproportionately affect students of color, students with disabilities, students with lower income backgrounds, English language learners, and other underserved groups.[160] Instead of tracking, successful middle schools enable a balance of collaborative and independent work that is appropriately challenging. They leverage personalized learning, cooperative learning, and varied groupings based on students' interest, skills, and choice, among others. Key to successful grouping in middle school is a commitment to assess student learning regularly and reassign groupings appropriately, thus ensuring inadvertent tracking does not occur.

Successful middle schools recognize that learning happens both within and beyond the school day and the school walls. They acknowledge that young adolescents' learning spaces vary widely and include the community, the home, and virtual environments. Successful middle schools translate the fundamental organizational structures of teaming, flexible scheduling, and varied grouping to distance, remote, hybrid, and online learning contexts. In doing so, regardless of the type of learning environment, they keep the academic development and personal growth of each student as the primary goal of middle level education.

I Am Poem

By Faye A., Grade 7

I Am

I am Faye

I am myself and only myself

Not the mask that covers my soul

Not the family I was born into

Not my culture, beliefs, or religion

Not my marks or IQ

I am who I choose to be

I am not defined by labels

The words girl, weak, ugly, and short are written all over me

Though no matter how hard I try to wash away the ink stains

They will never disappear

But that should not matter

For the ink is not visible to anyone who looks past it

What they see will be my true identity

Though you may not know me

My labels do not define me

It may take some time for you to see

But beneath this mask

I am me and only me

Me

Young Adolescent Development and Implications for Educators

During early adolescence, the developmental period from age 10 through 15, youth experience significant changes and rapid growth.[161] In fact, other than infancy, it is the greatest period of change in the human lifespan.[162] Being responsive to this growth and development has been the hallmark of middle level education since the field's inception.[163] Within the past two decades, however, this prominent reliance on a developmental perspective has been critiqued for the ways that it potentially limits understandings of young adolescents and often overlooks issues of equity, privilege, and power.[164] Within this section, young adolescent developmental characteristics are cautiously shared and grounded in four fundamental beliefs that both acknowledge the importance of developmentalism and critique an over-reliance on that perspective.

First, to be effective, schools for young adolescents must be developmentally responsive to their students. Teachers must understand students' cognitive abilities in order to create a curriculum that is challenging and stimulates engagement rather than one that leads to frustration and disengagement. Likewise, for educators to build student-teacher relationships that students deem to be safe, caring, and trusting, teachers must understand students' social-emotional needs. Designing a learning environment, building relationships, and creating lessons that consider students' developmental characteristics, along with being responsive to their social and cultural identities and experiences, are essential and enhance students' academic and overall well-being

Second, middle grades educators and researchers must exercise caution when discussing young adolescents holistically. Developmental characteristics should not be viewed as essentialized attributes where uniformity across or within young adolescents is assumed. Rather, developmental characteristics should be viewed as generalized traits, while acknowledging that a variety of environmental, cultural, and biological factors contribute to developmental differences between young adolescents.[165] Similarly, great variation and fluctuation in developmental traits can exist within an individual young adolescent. These fluctuations exist across context and time, meaning a student might be able to display higher cognitive functioning in one situation but not another.[166]

Third, middle grades educators should seek to understand each individual learner's developmental characteristics. Developmentally responsive education is most effective when it is based on a student's individual developmental characteristics, as opposed to those attributed to early adolescence overall. Generalizable understandings of young adolescents can be helpful and, at points, even necessary for school-wide and whole-class planning. However, due to the variations that exist between young adolescents, such decisions should be based on developmental commonalities of learners within that particular school or classroom while also accounting for and considering students whose developmental needs might be different.

Fourth, to create equitable schools, middle grades educators need to consider the ways that developmentalism may constrain our understanding of young adolescents. Middle school advocates should reflect on how this perspective can limit perceptions of youth and thereby actually work against the goal of creating self-actualized students.[167] Educators engaging in developmentally responsive practices need to observe whose voices, experiences, and identities are included and, conversely, not included. For example, until recently, a developmental perspective considered physical differences exclusively in terms of boys and girls. Responsive middle grades educators should recognize that relying on such a limited scope can cause damage and stress for students who are intersex, transgender, gender fluid, or gender non-conforming.

Relatedly, making meaning of students solely through developmentalism neglects the social realities that many youth experience. For example, research indicates that Black girls often experience adultification, or the assumption that they are older than their biological age.[168] The adultification of Black girls peaks between the ages of 10 and 14.[169] When adultification occurs, Black girls are perceived as less innocent than their White peers and, because they are not recognized as being their actual biological age, their developmental needs are not met. While such instances do not negate the relevance of developmental practices, as all youth deserve to have their developmental needs met, they do highlight the restrictions of exclusively using developmental traits to support and understand youth. An overly narrow perspective on young adolescent development leaves youth vulnerable and can contribute to inequitable outcomes, particularly for those with marginalized identities.

It is within the framework of these four fundamental beliefs that the physical, cognitive, social-emotional, and psychological characteristics of early adolescence are presented below. Though these traits are listed separately, they are not distinct. Young adolescent development is interconnected, with each characteristic affecting each other. Because of the ways that development is intertwined, many characteristics could easily fit into multiple categories and are subjectively placed.[170] In addition, the list of traits and the accompanying implications for educators are not exhaustive. This is largely due to the fact that research examining how social identities such as race, gender, and social class influence development in students ages 10 through 15 is limited.[171] It is beneficial to connect the research listed below with other social science research that explicitly explores the in- and out-of-school experiences of youth from diverse backgrounds to support a more nuanced and comprehensive understanding of young adolescents.

 Physical Development

Characteristics

- Changes in hormones signal the development of primary sex characteristics and secondary sex characteristics.
- Females typically begin puberty one or two years before males.

- Breast development and first menstruation starts for girls, while boys experience enlargement of testes and increased penis size.
- Pubic, underarm, and facial hair growth develops.
- Acne and body odor may start to develop due to oil and sweat glands beginning to function.
- Young adolescents' bones often grow more rapidly than muscles, which can cause lack of coordination and clumsiness.
- Young adolescents can experience physical growing pains of legs and joints when bones are not sufficiently protected by muscle and tendons.
- Growth spurts and fluctuations in basal metabolism can result in restlessness and fatigue.
- Growth in the size and thickness of the larynx creates voice changes. Both girls and boys experience these changes, though it is more pronounced in boys. Girls' voices typically drop around three tones while boys' tones can change significantly more. It is also common for boys to experience "cracks" or sharp fluctuations in their voices as the change occurs.
- Growth is sporadic. For example, some young adolescents experience changes in hair growth and voice changes within a short period of time, while others experience these changes over the course of a couple of years. Collectively, changes can be seen as growth patterns.
- The onset of puberty is associated with higher incidence of peer group sexual harassment.
- Changes during puberty can cause transgender and gender non-conforming youth great stress and anxiety. Some transgender youth take puberty blockers to prevent or delay the onset of puberty.

Implications for Educators

- Design lessons that build in opportunities for movement and avoid long periods of sitting.
- Incorporate various seating options for students, including differently-sized chairs and desks, couches, and seating that can move, such as wobble chairs.
- Provide hygiene bags for students who might need items such as deodorant and feminine products.

- Incorporate co-ed health education into the curriculum to help students develop an understanding of the changes in their bodies. Students need opportunities to ask questions about their physical changes of adults with whom they feel comfortable and deem trustworthy.

- Integrate conversations about sexual harassment and consent into the curriculum and be attentive to sexual harassment that students might experience. Have clear policies and procedures in place for students to report such harassment if it occurs.

- Interrupt deficit talk and negative comparisons regarding body image and standards of beauty, which can stem from young adolescents' increased awareness of their physical changes.

- Be attentive to eating disorders and self-harming.

- Avoid using gender binary language such as boys/girls and ladies/gentlemen. Ask students for the pronouns they use and commit to using them.

 # Cognitive Development

Characteristics

- Fundamental areas of the brain undergo significant development during early adolescence.

- Shifts from concrete thinking to an increased capability to engage in abstract thinking occur.

- Metacognition, or the ability to think about one's own thinking, starts to develop.

- Independent thought increases, as does the ability to debate different stances or positions.

- The ability to set personal goals and think about current and future needs is enhanced.

- Young adolescents are more interested to learn about topics they personally find relevant and interesting.

- The ability to engage in critical, analytical, and creative thinking increases, and students need opportunities to practice and develop these skills.

- Young adolescents enjoy using skills to solve real-life problems and prefer authentic learning experiences.
- Risk-taking increases and can be influenced by a tendency for sensation-seeking.
- Young adolescents develop and appreciate a more sophisticated and nuanced level of humor.
- Though young adolescents are influenced by stereotypes found in the media and learned in their homes, they have the ability to understand different perspectives and develop the ability to examine information objectively.
- By the end of early adolescence, most youth are able to perform cognitive control tasks at the same level as adults.

Implications for Educators

- Connect lessons to students' real-life experiences.
- Invite students to co-design learning opportunities around societal issues that pique their interest.
- Incorporate authentic learning experiences, such as service learning, that enables students to be actively and civically engaged.
- Provide opportunities for students to practice planning and decision making.
- Personalize lessons based on students' wide-ranging cognitive abilities and interest.
- Provide ongoing learning opportunities for students to engage in critical and creative thinking.
- Help students examine their own biases and assumptions as they self-reflect and consider different perspectives.
- Promote positive risk taking to support learning and growth.

 *Social-Emotional Development*

Characteristics

- While still seeking affirmation from their family and other important adults in their life, young adolescents have a strong desire to belong to a peer group.

- As friend groups become more important, exposure to both positive and negative peer pressure increases.

- Most incidents of bullying occur during early adolescence and can have a profound impact on students' well-being.

- Young adolescents can feel torn between fitting in with their peer groups while also trying to form their own independent identities.

- Young adolescents are often interested in popular culture and trends. In addition, social media usage increases as a way to connect with peers and the world at large.

- Though they continue to be influenced by family values, young adolescents increasingly model the behaviors of their peers, celebrity icons, and heroes.

- Fluctuation in emotions and behaviors occur, such as moments of anxiety and worry and instances of bravado and optimism.

- Young adolescents often feel their problems are unique to them and their emotions sometimes appear exaggerated to others.

- As young adolescents seek independence, their propensity for challenging adult authority can increase.

- Romantic and sexual attraction often develops. This includes same sex attraction, with 14 being around the average age that gay youth come out in the United States.

- A sizable minority of young adolescents engage in sexual behaviors.

- Young adolescents develop a deeper and more nuanced awareness and understanding of social injustices such as racism, sexism, and homophobia. This heightened awareness can be triggering and lead to racialized trauma for students from racially marginalized backgrounds.[172]

Implications for Educators

- Incorporate social-emotional learning into the curriculum to support the development of empathy and healthy peer relationships.

- Design learning opportunities that allow students to play out their emotions such as role play.

- Support students' abilities to relieve emotional stress in healthy ways.

- Offer spaces in the classroom or school building where students can take a moment to de-stress, reflect, or talk with an educator in a safe environment when needed, with no punitive intent.

- Implement middle school transition programs that can help ease the fear or anxiety that some young adolescents experience when starting a new school.

- Create opportunities for positive peer interactions through cooperative and collaborative learning experiences.

- Implement anti-bullying and anti-harassment programs and policies, as well as curriculum that teaches students how to become upstanders who intervene when bullying occurs.

- Avoid heteronormative language that assumes and sends a message that heterosexuality is the only sexual orientation.

- Acknowledge and commit to learning about the impact of systemic racism and racial trauma.[173]

- Elicit input from students to co-develop their own interventions for coping and healing.[174]

- Provide opportunities for students from historically marginalized backgrounds to tell their own stories about their experiences as a way of helping youth to develop their voices and critically examine their experiences in supportive, affirming, and safe spaces.[175]

Psychological Development

Characteristics

- During early adolescence, students often seek to find their own individuality, uniqueness, and autonomy. Central questions of exploration include Who am I? How do I see myself? How do my peers and adults see me? and How will I affect the world?

- Fluctuations in feelings of superiority and inferiority can occur as young adolescents engage in self-discovery.

- Young adolescents start to identify in multiple ways based on social context and environment. For example, they might act one way at home, and behave differently while with their peer groups in school or on social media.

- Young adolescents often desire autonomy, especially in personal matters such as hair styles and fashion choices.

- Young adolescents often inaccurately assume they have less autonomy than their peers.

- Young adolescents may begin to develop a passion for at least one hobby, sport, or interest that brings them joy and a sense of purpose. Sometimes students need help identifying such interests.

- Young adolescents often experience a deeper awareness of their social identities such as race, gender, social class, religion, sexuality, and immigration status. Having a strong and positive connection to their social identities is important for their social and academic well-being. Though this is true for all youth, this is particularly true for students with marginalized social identities.

- Young adolescents benefit from a nuanced and multifaceted understanding of identity that goes beyond stereotypical expectations of group norms.

Implications for Educators

- Build opportunities for identity exploration into the curriculum, both within traditional academic classes and through exploratory classes where students might be introduced to new interests and future passions.

- Support students with their digital identity development by implementing a digital citizenship curriculum that incorporates conversations about the use of social media.[176]

- Create personalized learning pathways for students.

- Support students' self-reflection in constructive and healthy ways.

- Adopt school structures such as advisory programs that ensure that each student has one adult that knows them well and can support their positive identity development.

- Offer school programming such as Gay-Straight Alliances and other affinity clubs that allow students safer places to build community, challenge stereotypes, discuss issues facing them in and out of school, and cultivate leadership skills by raising awareness about issues most important to them.

- Validate and affirm young adolescents' feelings and experiences, even if some of their concerns might seem trivial to adults.

- Create psychological safe environments for young adolescents to discuss their emotions and experiences.[177]

- Avoid taking a colorblind approach to teaching as it becomes difficult to support young adolescents to develop a strong sense of self when students' cultural and linguistic backgrounds are not acknowledged.

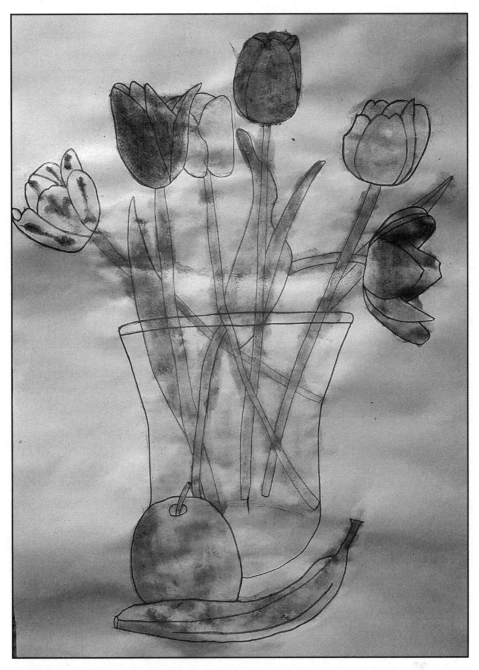

Untitled _by Elisabeth L., Grade 7_

Every flower blossoms the way it wishes to blossom. Every stem leans in its own unique direction. All of the objects are part of one image. They all have a part in the picture, without one it would feel incomplete. This is what we are part of. A community.

Bobcat Pride by Rephael S, Grade 7

Our Middle School's mascot is a Bobcat, and I wanted to bring all of the clubs and activities together that help us show our Bobcat Pride. In my collage, I added our school's sports which includes basketball, soccer, softball, football, wrestling, tennis, bowling, volleyball, cheer, track and field, cross country, and hockey. To the right I added the arts/clubs which includes Drama, Movie Club, Band, Orchestra, Yearbook, Environmental, Debate, Broadway Appreciation, Singing, Art, Animal Lovers, Math Counts, Robotics, Stage Crew, Dungeons and Dragons, Gaming, TV and Me, Story Writers and Marketing Club. We also have the Gay Straight Alliance (GSA) and the Student Government Association (SGA). Lastly, the triangles represent what each person looks like as an individual, but also as a community.

A Historical Account

In the midst of an emerging middle school movement, National Middle School Association (now AMLE) was started in 1973 by a group of college professors and middle level educators who saw a need for a national organization specifically focused on the education of young adolescents, ages 10 to 15. They convened annual conferences, published a few resources, and launched *Middle School Journal*. However, they realized no single comprehensive statement answered the frequently asked question, "Just what is a middle school?"

John Swaim, 1980 president of National Middle School Association, believed NMSA could answer this important question and appointed a committee to prepare a position paper, which resulted in the 1982 publication of the original *This We Believe*. This document became a living document that would periodically be reviewed, revised, and even re-conceptualized to represent what evolving research and practice tell us about educating young adolescents.

In this fifth edition of the association's position paper, we wish to honor the commitment and vision of individuals engaged in the development of prior editions:

1982: *This We Believe*
Committee members: Alfred A. Arth, William Alexander, Charles Cherry, Donald Eichhorn, Conrad Toepfer, and Gordon Vars. Editor: John Lounsbury.

1995: *This We Believe: Developmentally Responsive Middle Level Schools*
Committee members: John Arnold, Sherrel Bergmann, Barbara Brodhagen, Ross Burkhardt, Maria Garza- Lubeck, John Lounsbury, Marion Payne, Chris Stevenson, Sue Swaim, and Gordon Vars. Writing Team: Ross Burkhardt, Gordon Vars, John Lounsbury, and Sue Swaim.

2003: *This We Believe: Successful Schools for Young Adolescents*
Committee members: Edward Brazee, Deborah Kasak, John Lounsbury, Gert Nesin, Charles Palmer, Linda Robinson, Sue Swaim, and Phyllis Toy Wong. Writing Team: Sue Swaim, John Lounsbury, and Edward Brazee. A companion document, *Research and Resources in Support of This We Believe*, prepared by AMLE's Research Committee headed by Vincent A. Anfara, Jr., was released concurrently.

2010: *This We Believe: Keys to Educating Young Adolescents*
Committee members: Gayle Andrews, Jack Berckemeyer, Edward Brazee, Brenda Cassellius, Betty Edwards, Annette Fante, Bill Ferriter, Mark Springer, Sue Swaim, April Tibbles, Chris Toy, and Janet Vernon. Writing Team: Edward Brazee, John Lounsbury, Mark Springer, and Sue Swaim. A companion document, *Research and Resources in Support of This We Believe*, prepared by AMLE's Research Committee headed by Micki M. Caskey was released concurrently.

With Gratitude

This book was made possible by the collective, conscientious, and caring efforts of many. AMLE is indebted to the following individuals for their time, attention, and support of the development of this edition of AMLE's foundational position paper, *The Successful Middle School: This We Believe.*

Thank you to our students!

We selected poetry, art, and quotes from more than 100 submissions made to our Student Voice initiative. Thanks to all students who shared their ideas and creativity!

Endnotes

1   Balfanz, R. (2009). *Putting middle grades students on the graduation path: A policy and practice brief.* National Middle School Association. https://www.amle.org/portals/0/pdf/articles/policy_brief_balfanz.pdf

      Balfanz, R., Herzog, L., & Mac Iver, D.J. (2007). Preventing student disengagement and keeping students on the graduation path in urban middle-grades schools: Early identification and effective interventions, *Educational Psychologist, 42*(4), 223-235. https://doi.org/10.1080/00461520701621079

2   Kansky, J., Allen, J.P., & Diener, E. (2016). Early adolescent affect predicts later life outcomes. *Applied Psychology: Health and Well-Being, 8*(2), 192-212. https://doi.org/10.1111/aphw.12068

3   Balfanz, R. (2009). *Putting middle grades students on the graduation path: A policy and practice brief.* National Middle School Association. https://www.amle.org/portals/0/pdf/articles/policy_brief_balfanz.pdf

      Camera, W., O'Connor, R., Mattern, K., & Hanson, M.A. (Eds.) (2015). Beyond academics: A holistic framework for enhancing education and workplace success. ACT, Inc. http:// www.act.org/content/act/en/research/beyond-academics.html?page=0&chapter=0

4   Williams, J., Mims, L., & Johnson, H. (2019). *Young adolescent development* (Remaking Middle School Working Paper series).Youth-Nex Center, University of Virginia. https://drive.google.com/file/d/1pY5hM18aKBSDCWxYpx4XnxasMKUeyyy-/view

5   ibid

6   Orfield, Frankenberg, Ee, & Cuscera, 2014, cited in Williams, J., Mims, L., & Johnson, H. (2019). *Young adolescent development* (Remaking Middle School Working Paper series). Youth-Nex Center, University of Virginia. https://drive.google.com/file/d/1pY5hM18aKBSDCWxYpx4XnxasMKUeyyy-/view

7   Gopalan, M. & Nelson, A.A. (2019). Understanding the racial discipline gap in schools. *AERA Open, 5*(2).

8   Kosciw, J.G., Greytak, E. A., Bartkiewicz, M. J., Boesen, M. J., & Palmer, N. A. (2012). *The 2011 national school climate survey: The experiences of lesbian, gay, bisexual and transgender youth in our nation's schools.* GLSEN.

      Kosciw, J. G., Greytak, E. A., & Diaz, E. M. (2009). Who, what, where, when, and why: Demographic and ecological factors contributing to hostile school climate for lesbian, gay, bisexual, and transgender youth. *Journal of Youth Adolescence, 38*(1), 976-988. https:/doi.org/10.1007/s10964-009-9412-1

9   Manning, M. L. (2000). A brief history of the middle school. *The Clearing House, 73*(4), 192-192.

10   Alexander, W. (1963). *The junior high school: A changing view.* Cornell University.

11   Erb, T.O., & Stevenson, C. (1999) What difference does teaming make?, *Middle School Journal, 30*(3), 47-50. https://doi.org/10.1080/00940771.1999.11494587

      Felner, R.D., Jackson, A.W., Kasak, D., Mulhall, P., Brand, S., & Flowers, N. (1997). The impact of school reform for the middle years: Longitudinal study of a network engaged in Turning Points-based comprehensive school transformation. *Phi Delta Kappan, 78*, 528–532, 541–550.

12   Carolan, B. V., Weiss, C. C., & Matthews, J. S. (2013). Which middle school model works best? Evidence from the early childhood longitudinal study. *Youth & Society, 47*(5), 591–614. https://doi.org/10.1177/0044118X13478625

Hong, K., Zimmer, R., & Engberg, J. (2018). How does grade configuration impact student achievement in elementary and middle school grades?, *Journal of Urban Economics, Elsevier, 105*(C), 1-19.

13 Williams, J., Mims, L., & Johnson, H. (2019). *Young adolescent development* (Remaking Middle School Working Paper series).Youth-Nex Center, University of Virginia. https://drive.google.com/file/d/1pY5hM18aKBSDCWxYpx4XnxasMKUeyyy-/view

Bishop, P.A., & Downes, J.M. (2019). *Optimizing teaching and learning in the middle grades.* (Remaking Middle School Working Paper series, Youth-Nex Center, University of Virginia). https://drive.google.com/file/d/1c009BXixwb4YjRkZlkR66GgjcwnVuLH4/view

14 Scales, P. C., Boekel, M. V., Pekel, K., Syvertsen, A. K., & Roehlkepartain, E. C. (2020). Effects of developmental relationships with teachers on middle-school students' motivation and performance. *Psychology in the Schools, 57*(4), 646–677. https://doi.org/10.1002/pits.22350

15 Gray, D. L., Hope, E. C., & Matthews, J. S. (2018). Black and belonging at school: A case for interpersonal, instructional, and institutional opportunity structures. *Educational Psychologist, 53*(2), 97-113.

Kiefer, S. M., Alley, K. M., & Ellerbrock, C. R. (2015). Teacher and peer support for young adolescents' motivation, engagement, and school belonging. *RMLE Online, 38*(8), 1–18. https://doi.org/10.1080/19404476.2015.11641184

Sakiz, G., Pape, S. J., & Hoy, A. W. (2012). Does perceived teacher affective support matter for middle school students in mathematics classrooms? *Journal of School Psychology, 50*, 235–255.

16 Tillery, A. D., Varjas, K., Roach, A. T., Kuperminc, G. P., & Meyers, J. (2013). The importance of adult connections in adolescents' sense of school belonging: Implications for schools and practitioners. *Journal of School Violence, 12*(2), 134–155. https://doi.org/10.1080/15388220.2012.762518

Nichols, S. L. (2008). An exploration of students' belongingness beliefs in one middle school. *The Journal of Experimental Education, 76*(2), 145–169. https://doi.org/10.3200/JEXE.76.2.145-169

17 Bouchard, K. L., & Berg, D. H. (2017). Students' school belonging: Juxtaposing the perspectives of teachers and students in the late elementary school years (grades 4–8). *School Community Journal, 27*(1), 107–136.

18 Harrison, L. M., Hurd, E., & Brinegar, K. M. (2019). Exploring the convergence of developmentalism and cultural responsiveness. In K. M. Brinegar, L. M. Harrison, & E. Hurd (Eds.), *Equity & cultural responsiveness in the middle grades* (pp. 3-23). Information Age Publishing.

19 Gibbs-Grey, T., & Harrison, L.M., (in press). Call me worthy: Utilizing storytelling to reclaim narratives about Black middle school girls experiencing inequitable school discipline. *Equity & Excellence in Education.*

20 Rawls, J., & Robinson, J. (2019). *Youth culture power: A #HipHopEd guide to building teacher-student relationships and increasing student engagement.* Peter Lang.

21 Smith, M. L., Strahan, D., Patterson, B., Bouton, B., & McGaughey, N. (2018). Developmental aspects of young adolescents. In S. B. Mertens & M. M. Caskey (Eds.), *Literature reviews in support of the middle level education research agenda* (pp. 3-24). Information Age Publishing.

22 Minor, C. (2019). *We got this: Equity, access, and the quest to be who our students need us to be.* Heinemann.

Reyes, C. C. (2019). Practicing "unsettled listening" to the migration narratives of young adolescent refugees. *Middle School Journal, 50*(4), 16-25. https://doi.org/10.1080/00940771.2019.1650546

23 Craig, S. E., & Sporleder, J. (2017). *Trauma-sensitive schools for the adolescent years: Promoting resiliency and healing, grades 6–12.* Teachers College Press.

Crosby, S. D., Howell, P., & Thomas, S. (2018). Social justice education through trauma-informed teaching. *Middle School Journal, 49*(4), 15–23. https://doi.org/10.1080/00940771.2018.1488470

Simmons, D. (2019). Why we can't afford whitewashed social-emotional learning. *ASCD Education Update, 61*(4), 2-3

24 DeMink-Carthew, J. (2018). Learning to teach in a "World Not Yet Finished": Social justice education in the middle level preservice teacher classroom. *Middle School Journal, 49*(4), 24–34. https://doi.org/10.1080/00940771.2018.1488471

Love, B.L. (2019). *We want to do more than survive: Abolitionist teaching and the pursuit of educational freedom.* Beacon Press.

25 Kiefer, S. M., & Ellerbrock, C. (2020). Supporting young adolescent motivation in school through an adolescent-centered community of care. In D. Virtue (Ed.), *International handbook of middle level education, theory, research, and policy* (pp. 161-179). Routledge.

Ruzek, E. A., Hafen, C. A., Allen, J. P., Gregory, A., Mikami, A. Y., & Pianta, R. C. (2016). How teacher emotional support motivates students: The mediating roles of perceived peer relatedness, autonomy support, and competence. *Learning and Instruction, 42*, 95-103.

26 Kiefer, S. M., Alley, K. M., & Ellerbrock, C. R. (2015). Teacher and peer support for young adolescents' motivation, engagement, and school belonging. *RMLE Online, 38*(8), 1–18. https://doi.org/10.1080/19404476.2015.11641184

27 Fite, P. J., Poquiz, J., Díaz, K. I., Williford, A., & Tampke, E. C. (2019). Links between peer victimization, perceived school safety, and internalizing symptoms in middle childhood. *School Psychology Review, 48*(4), 309–319. https://doi.org/10.17105/SPR-2018-0092.V48-4

Morrow, M. T., Hubbard, J. A., & Sharp, M. K. (2019). Preadolescents' internal attributions for negative peer experiences: Links to child and classroom peer victimization and friendship. *Journal of Abnormal Child Psychology, 47*(3), 393-404.

Studer, J. R., & Mynatt, B. S. (2015). Bullying prevention in middle schools: a collaborative approach. *Middle School Journal, 46*(3), 25-32. https://doi.org/10.1080/00940771.2015.11461912

28 Wellenreiter, B. R. (2018). Hallways paved with good intentions: Analyzing rules and procedures in non-classroom middle school spaces. *Middle School Journal, 49*(2), 10-15. https://doi.org/10.1080/00940771.2017.1413272

29 Lewis, J. A., Nishina, A., Hall, A. R., Cain, S., Bellmore, A., & Witkow, M. R. (2018). Early adolescents' peer experiences with ethnic diversity in middle school: Implications for academic outcomes. *Journal of Youth and Adolescence, 47*(1), 194-206.

Van Ryzin, M. J., & Roseth, C. J. (2018). Cooperative learning in middle school: A means to improve peer relations and reduce victimization, bullying, and related outcomes. *Journal of Educational Psychology, 110*(8), 1192.

30 Killen, M., Mulvey, K.L. , & Hitti, A. (2012). Social exclusion in childhood: A developmental intergroup perspective. *Child Development, 84*(3), 772–790. https://doi.org/10.1111/cdev.12012

Killen, M , & Rutland A (2011). *Children and social exclusion: Morality, prejudice, and group identity.* Wiley-Blackwell.

31 Downing. B. (2019). Middle (mis)management: Staff sanctioned victimization in the middle grades. In K. M. Brinegar, L. M. Harrison, & E. Hurd (Eds.), *Equity & cultural responsiveness in the middle grades* (pp. 113-131). Information Age Publishing.

32 Pica-Smith, C., & Poynton, T. A. (2014). Supporting interethnic and interracial friendships among youth to reduce prejudice and racism in schools: The role of the school counselor. *Professional School Counseling, 18*(1), 86-89.

33   Hart Barnett, J. E., Fisher, K. W., O'Connell, N., & Franco, K. (2019). Promoting upstander behavior to address bullying in schools. *Middle School Journal, 50*(1), 6–11. https://doi.org/10.1080/00940771.2018.1550377

34   Gibson, E. L., & Barr, R. D. (2017). Building a culture of hope: Exploring implicit biases against poverty. *National Youth-At-Risk Journal, 2*(2), 39-50.

Staats, C. (2016). Understanding implicit bias: What educators should know. *American Educator, 39*(4), 29-43.

Warikoo, N., Sinclair, S., Fei, J., & Jacoby-Senghor, D. (2016). Examining racial bias in education: A new approach. *Educational Researcher, 45*(9), 508-514.

35   Staats, C. (2016). Understanding implicit bias: What educators should know. *American Educator, 39*(4), 29-43.

36   Carter Andrews, D. J., & Gutwein, M. (2020). Middle school students' experiences with inequitable discipline practices in school: The elusive quest for cultural responsiveness. *Middle School Journal, 51*(1), 29-38. https://doi.org/10.1080/00940771.2019.1689778

Walker, B. L. T. (2020). "Loud, proud, and love a crowd:" African American girls and school discipline practices. *Middle School Journal, 51*(1), 12-18. https://doi.org/10.1080/00940771.2019.1689776

37   Williams, J., Mims, L., & Johnson, H. (2019). *Young adolescent development* (Remaking Middle School Working Paper series).Youth-Nex Center, University of Virginia. https://drive.google.com/file/d/1pY5hM18aKBSDCWxYpx4XnxasMKUeyyy-/view

Chang, E. S., Greenberger, E., Chen, C., Heckhausen, J., & Farruggia, S. P. (2010). Nonparental adults as social resources in the transition to adulthood. *Journal of Research on Adolescence, 20*(4), 1065–1082. https://doi.org/10.1111/j.1532-7795.2010.00662.x

Griffith, A. N., & Larson, R. W. (2016). Why trust matters: How confidence in leaders transforms what adolescents gain from youth programs. *Journal of Research on Adolescence, 26*(4), 790–804. https://doi.org/10.1111/jora.12230

Hurd, N. M., & Zimmerman, M. A. (2014). An Analysis of natural mentoring relationship profiles and associations with mentees' mental health: Considering links via support from important others. *American Journal of Community Psychology, 53*(1–2), 25–36. https://doi.org/10.1007/s10464-013-9598-y

Okonofua, J. A., Paunesku, D., & Walton, G. M. (2016). Brief intervention to encourage empathic discipline cuts suspension rates in half among adolescents. *Proceedings of the National Academy of Sciences, 113*(19), 5221-5226.

Oyserman, D., Brickman, D., & Rhodes, M. (2007). School success, possible selves, and parent school involvement. *Family Relations, 56*(5), 479-489.

38   Bennett, C.A., & Martin, K. (2018). Reclaiming advisory: Advocacy in action. *Middle School Journal, 49*(1), 32-37. https://doi.org/10.1080/00940771.2018.1399330

39   Shulkind, S.B., & Foote, J. (2009). Creating a culture of connectedness through middle school advisory programs. *Middle School Journal, 41*(1), 20-27. https://doi.org/10.1080/00940771.2009.11461700

40   Boonk, L, Gijselaers, H., Ritzen, H., Brand-Gruwel, S. (2018). A review of the relationship between parental involvement indicators and academic achievement. *Educational Research Review, 24*, 10-30.

Also: Mo, Y., & Singh, K. (2008). Parents' relationships and involvement: Effects on students' school engagement and performance. *RMLE Online, 31*(10). http://www.amle.org/portals/0/pdf/rmle/rmle_vol31_no10.pdf

41   Cobbina, J.E., Galasso, M., Cunningham, M., Melde, C., & Heinze, J. (2019) A qualitative study of perception of school safety among youth in a high crime city. *Journal of School Violence, 19*(3), 277-291. https://doi.org/10.1080/15388220.2019.1677477

42 Hong, J. S., Voisin, D. R., & Lee, J. (2016). Urban African American youth and their caregivers' perceptions of school safety in Chicago: A social-ecological perspective. *Youth Violence and Juvenile Justice, 16*(2), 174–189. https://doi.org/10.1177/1541204016680406

43 Mallett, C. A. (2017). The school-to-prison pipeline: Disproportionate impact on vulnerable children and adolescents. *Education and Urban Society, 49*(6), 563–592. https://doi.org/10.1177/0013124516644053

44 Schiff, M. (2018). Can restorative justice disrupt the "school-to-prison pipeline"? *Contemporary Justice Review, 21*(2), 121-139. https://doi.org/10.1080/10282580.2018.1455509

Gregory, A., Huang, F.L., Anyon, Y., Greer, E., & Downing, B. (2018) An examination of restorative interventions and racial equity in out-of-school suspensions. *School Psychology Review, 47*(2), 167-182. https://doi.org/10.17105/SPR-2017-0073.V47-2

45 Winn, M. T. (2018). *Justice on both sides: Transforming education through restorative justice.* Harvard Education Press.

46 Owens, E.G. (2017) Testing the school-to-prison pipeline. *Journal of Policy Analysis and Management, 36*(1), 11-37.

47 Mack, D. (2019). *Student perception of safety and positive school climate after trauma informed care professional development.* (Doctoral dissertation, Bowling Green State University). https://etd.ohiolink.edu/pg_10?::NO:10:P10_ETD_SUBID:182938

48 Russell, S. T., & Fish, J. N. (2016). Mental health in lesbian, gay, bisexual, and transgender (LGBT) youth. *Annual Review of Clinical Psychology, 12*, 465–487. https://doi.org/10.1146/annurev-clinpsy-021815-093153

49 Li, G., Wu, A.D., Marshall, S.K., Watson, R,J., Adjei, J.K., Park, M., Saewyc, E.M. (2019). Investigating site-level longitudinal effects of population health interventions: Gay-Straight Alliances and school safety. *SSM Population Health, 7*. https://doi.org/10.1016/j.ssmph.2019.100350

Poteat, V.P., Sinclair, K.O., DiGiovanni, C.D., Koenig, B.W., & Russell, S.T. (2013). Gay-straight alliances are associated with student health: A multischool comparison of LGBTQ and heterosexual youth. *Journal of Research on Adolescence, 23*(2), 319-330.

Russell, S.T., & Fish, J.N. (2016). Mental health in lesbian, gay, bisexual, and transgender (LGBT) youth. *Annual Review of Clinical Psychology, 12*, 465-487.

50 Umaña-Taylor, A. J., Quintana, S. M., Lee, R. M., Cross, W. E., Jr., Rivas-Drake, D., Schwartz, S. J., Syed, M., Yip, T., & Seaton, E. (2014). Ethnic and racial identity during adolescence and into young adulthood: An integrated conceptualization. *Child Development, 85*, 21–39. https://doi.org/10.1111/cdev.12196

51 Brittian Loyd, A., & Williams, B.V. (2016). The potential for youth programs to promote African American youth's development of ethnic and racial identity. *Child Development Perspectives, 11*, 29-38. https://doi.org/10.1111/cdep.12204

Jones, J. M., Lee, L. H., Matlack, A., & Zigarelli, J. (2018). Using sisterhood networks to cultivate ethnic identity and enhance school engagement. *Psychology in the Schools, 55*(1), 20-35.

Brown, D. F., & Leaman, H. L. (2007). Recognizing and responding to young adolescents' ethnic identity development. In S. B. Mertens, V. A. Anfara, & M. M. Caskey (Eds.), *The young adolescent and the middle school.* Information Age Publishing.

52 Borman, G.D., Rozek, C.S., Pyne, J., Hanselman, P. (2019). Reappraising academic and social adversity improves middle school students' academic achievement, behavior, and well-being. *Proceedings of the National Academy of Sciences, 116*(33), 16286–16291 https://doi.org/10.1073/pnas.1820317116

53 Gilewski, C. D., & Nunn, M. L. (2016). *Research summary: Transitioning young adolescents from elementary to middle schools.* Association for Middle Level Education. http://www.amle.org/ServicesEvents/ResearchSummary/TabId/622/ArtMID/2112/ArticleID/750/Transitioning-Young-Adolescents-from-Elementary-to-Middle-School.aspx

Andrews, C., & Bishop, P. (2012). Middle grades transition programs around the globe. *Middle School Journal, 44*(1), 8-14. https://doi.org/10.1080/00940771.2012.11461834

54 Pate, P. E., & Andrews, P. G. (2006). *Research summary: Parent involvement.* Association for Middle Level Education. http://www.amle.org/TabId/270/ArtMID/888/ArticleID/328/Research-Summary-Parent-Involvement.aspx

55 Smith, T. E., Reinke, W. M., Herman, K. C., & Huang, F. (2019). Understanding family–school engagement across and within elementary- and middle-school contexts. *School Psychology, 34*(4), 363–375. https://doi.org/10.1037/spq0000290

56 Allen, J., Tucker, E. Y., & Newsome, M. E. (2013). Family-school partnerships. In P.G. Andrews (Ed.), *Research to guide practice in middle grades education* (pp. 437-466).Association for Middle Level Education.

57 Fenton, P., Ocasio-Stoutenburg, L., & Harry, B. (2017). The power of parent engagement: Sociocultural considerations in the quest for equity, *Theory Into Practice, 56*(3), 214-225. https://doi.org/10.1080/00405841.2017.1355686

58 Kim, Y. (2009). Minority parental involvement and school barriers: Moving the focus away from deficiencies of parents. *Educational Research Review, 4*(2), 80–102. https://doi.org/10.1016/j.edurev.2009.02.003

59 Bower, H. A., & Griffin, D. (2011). Can the Epstein model of parental involvement work in a high-minority, high-poverty elementary school? A case study. *Professional School Counseling, 15*(2), 77–87.

    Curry, K. A., & Holter, A. (2019). The influence of parent social networks on parent perceptions and motivation for involvement. *Urban Education, 54*(4), 535–563.

    Ho, P., & Cherng, H. S. (2018). How far can the apple fall? Differences in teacher perceptions of minority and immigrant parents and their impact on academic outcomes. *Social Science Research, 74*, 132-145.

60 Hill, N. E., Witherspoon, D. P., & Bartz, D. (2018). Parental involvement in education during middle school: Perspectives of ethnically diverse parents, teachers, and students. *The Journal of Educational Research, 111*(1), 12-27.

    Rodríguez-Castro, M., Salas, S., & Murray, B. (2016). You say, "cariño"; I say, "caring": Latino newcomer immigrant families in the middle. *Middle School Journal, 47*(5), 14–20. https://doi.org/10.1080/00940771.2016.1226644

61 Kim, Y. (2009). Minority parental involvement and school barriers: Moving the focus away from deficiencies of parents. *Educational Research Review, 4*(2), 80–102. https://doi.org/10.1016/j.edurev.2009.02.003

62 Greene, S. (2013). Mapping low-income African American parents' roles in their children's education in a changing political economy. *Teachers College Record, 115*(1), 1–33.

    Kyzar, K., & Jimerson, J. B. (2018). Bridging the school-home divide in the middle grades: A process for strengthening school-family partnerships. *Middle School Journal, 49*(1), 13-23. https://doi.org/10.1080/00940771.2018.1399331

63 Epstein, J. L. (2005). School-initiated family and community partnerships. In T. Erb (Ed.), *This we believe in action: Implementing successful middle level schools* (pp. 77–96). National Middle School Association.

    Kyzar, K., & Jimerson, J. B. (2018). Bridging the school-home divide in the middle grades: A process for strengthening school-family partnerships. *Middle School Journal, 49*(1), 13–23. https://doi.org/10.1080/00940771.2018.1399331

64 Rodríguez-Castro, M., Salas, S., & Benson, T. (2018). To Google Translate™ or not? Newcomer Latino communities in the middle. *Middle School Journal, 49*(2), 3-9. https://doi.org/10.1080/00940771.2017.1413270

65   Haines, S. J., Gross, J. M., Blue-Banning, M., Francis, G. L., & Turnbull, A. P. (2015). Fostering family–school and community–school partnerships in inclusive schools: Using practice as a guide. *Research and Practice for Persons with Severe Disabilities, 40*(3), 227-239.

66   Blank, M. J., Jacobson, R., & Melaville, A. (2012). *Achieving results through community school partnerships: How district and community leaders are building effective, sustainable relationships.* Center for American Progress.

67   Coffey, H., & Fulton, S. (2018). The responsible change project: Building a justice-oriented middle school curriculum through critical service-learning. *Middle School Journal, 49*(5), 16-25. https://doi.org/10.1080/00940771.2018.1509560

Guffey, S. K., Parrish, C. W., Ferguson, S. N., & Green, A. M. (2020). Successes and challenges of a summer STEM program for students from Title I schools. *Middle School Journal, 51*(3), 26-32. https://doi.org/10.1080/00940771.2020.1735869

Solomon, S., & Schaefer, M. B. (2019). From the schoolyard to the campus: Helping middle grades students see themselves as future college students. *Middle School Journal, 50*(1), 33-41. https://doi.org/10.1080/00940771.2018.1550376

68   Dani, D. (2019). A community and place-based approach to middle childhood science teacher education, *Middle School Journal, 50*(2), 45-52. https://doi.org/10.1080/00940771.2019.1576581

69   Blank, M. J., Jacobson, R., & Melaville, A. (2012). *Achieving results through community school partnerships: How district and community leaders are building effective, sustainable relationships.* Center for American Progress.

70   Edge, K., & Khamsi, K. (2012). International school partnerships as a vehicle for global education: Student perspectives. *Asia Pacific Journal of Education, 32*(4), 455-472.

71   Paris, D., & Alim, H. S. (Eds.). (2017). *Culturally sustaining pedagogies: Teaching and learning for justice in a changing world.* Teachers College Press.

72   Conklin, H. G., & Kalchman, M. (2018). Tensions of developing an exemplar middle grades teacher preparation program. In P. B. Howell, S. A. Faulkner, J. P. Jones, & J. Carpenter (Eds.), *Preparing middle level educators for 21st century schools* (pp. 5–28). Information Age Publishing.

Ochanji, M. K., Chen, R.-J., Daniels, E., Deringer, M. L., & McDaniel, J. (2016). A different kind of kid, a different kind of teacher education: Middle grades teachers reflect on their preparation to teach young adolescents. *Middle Grades Review, 2*(1), 1–17.

Pinter, H. H., Winter, K. K., & Strahan, D. (2017). Strengthening developmental trajectories toward responsiveness: Learning to teach at the middle-level. *Middle School Journal, 48*(5), 3-13. https://doi.org/10.1080/00940771.2017.1368313

Van Overschelde, J. P., Saunders, J. M., & Ash, G. E. (2017). "Teaching is a lot more than just showing up to class and grading assignments": Preparing middle-level teachers for longevity in the profession. *Middle School Journal, 48*(5), 28-38. https://doi.org/10.1080/00940771.2017.1368319

73   Jagla, V., Winter, K., Wall, A., Bickmore, D., Haverback, H.R., & Kemp-Graham, K. (2016). Educator development. In S. B. Mertens & M. M. Caskey (Eds.), *Literature reviews in support of the middle level education research agenda* (pp. 81-110). Information Age Publishing.

McEwin, K. & Smith, T. W. (2013) The professional preparation of middle grades teachers. In P.G. Andrews (Ed.), *Research to guide practice in middle grades education* (pp. 437-466). Association for Middle Level Education.

74   Jackson, A., & Davis, G. A. (2000). *Turning points 2000: Educating adolescents in the 21st century.* Teachers College Press.

75   Howell, P. B., Carpenter, J., & Jones, J. (Eds.). (2016). *Clinical preparation at the middle level: Practices and possibilities.* Information Age Publishing.

Harrison, L. M., Walls, C., & Hawk, R. (2016). Creating meaningful partnerships: Connecting teaching candidates with professional development schools through service learning. *School-University Partnerships, 9*(2), 40-49.

Harrison, L. M., & Keifer Kennedy, M. (2016). Supporting middle level students, teacher candidates, and teachers through forming professional developmental school partnerships. In P. B. Howell, J. Carpenter, & J. P. Jones (Eds.), *Clinical preparation at the middle level: Practices and possibilities* (pp. 59-77). Information Age Publishing.

76 Dani, D. (2019). A community and place-based approach to middle childhood science teacher education. *Middle School Journal, 50*(2), 45-52. https://doi.org/10.1080/00940771.2019.1576581

Harrison, L. M. (2013). Service learning and its impact on middle level preservice teachers' learning from field experiences. *Middle Grades Research Journal, 8*(3), 23-38.

77 Andrews, P. G., Moulton, M. J., & Hughes, H. E. (2018). Integrating social justice into middle grades teacher education. *Middle School Journal, 49*(5), 4-15. https://doi.org/10.1080/00940771.2018.1509562

Harrison, L. M., Gibbs-Grey, T., Dani, D., Kopish, M., Felton, M., Sprecher, K., & Bates, P. (2018). A collaborative approach to supporting middle childhood social justice teacher education. In P. B. Howell, S. A. Faulkner, & J. Carpenter, (Eds.), *Preparing middle level educators for 21st century schools: Enduring beliefs, changing times, evolving practices* (pp. 229 – 254). Information Age Publishing.

78 Andrews, D. J. C., Brown, T., Castillo, B. M., Jackson, D., & Vellanki, V. (2019). Beyond damage-centered teacher education: Humanizing pedagogy for teacher educators and preservice teachers. *Teachers College Record, 121*(4), 1-28.

79 Zeichner, K. M. (2009). *Teacher education and the struggle for social justice.* Routledge.

80 DeMink-Carthew, J., & Bishop, P. A. (2017). Passion is not enough: Preparing middle level preservice teachers to be advocates for change. *Middle School Journal, 48*(2), 14–23. https://doi.org/10.1080/00940771.2017.1272914

81 Howell, P. B., Cook, C. M., Miller, N. C., Thompson, N. L., Faulkner, S. A., & Rintamaa, M. F. (2018). The complexities of middle level teacher credentialing: Status report and future directions. *RMLE Online, 41*(4), 1–12. https://doi.org/10.1080/19404476.2018.1456840

82 Jagla, V., Winter, K., Wall, A., Bickmore, D., Haverback, H.R., & Kemp-Graham, K. (2016). Educator development. In S. B. Mertens & M. M. Caskey (Eds.), *Literature reviews in support of the middle level education research agenda* (pp. 10-14). Information Age Publishing.

83 Jackson, P.W. (1968). *Life in classrooms.* Holt, Rinehart, and Winston.

84 Kohli, R., Pizarro, M., & Nevárez, A. (2017). The "new racism" of K–12 schools: Centering critical research on racism. *Review of Research in Education, 41*(1), 182–202. https://doi.org/10.3102/0091732X16686949

85 Davis, C. L., & Hall, L. M. (2020). Spoken word performance as activism: Middle school poets challenge American racism. *Middle School Journal, 51*(2), 6-15. https://doi.org/10.1080/00940771.2019.1709256

Nojan, S. (2020). Why ethnic studies? Building critical consciousness among middle school students. *Middle School Journal, 51*(2), 25–35. https://doi.org/10.1080/00940771.2019.1709259

86 Schlechty, P. (2011). *Engaging students: The next level of working on the work.* Jossey-Bass.

87 Beane, J. A. (1997). *Curriculum integration: Designing the core of democratic education.* Teachers College Press.

88 Darling-Hammond, L., Friedlaender, D., & Snyder, J. (2014). *Student-centered schools: Policy supports for closing the opportunity gap.* Stanford Center for Opportunity Policy in Education. https://edpolicy.stanford.edu/sites/default/files/scope-pub-student-centered-policy.pdf

89 Harrison, L. M., Hurd, E., & Brinegar, K. (2020). *Integrative and interdisciplinary curriculum in the middle school.* Routledge.

90 Farber, K. & Bishop, P. (2018). Service learning in the middle grades: Learning by doing and caring, *RMLE Online, 41*(2), 1-15. https://doi.org/10.1080/19404476.2017.1415600

91 ibid

92 Minor, C. (2019). *We got this: Equity, access, and the quest to be who our students need us to be.* Heinemann.

93 Brinegar, K., & Bishop, P.A. (2011). Student learning and engagement in the context of curriculum integration. *Middle Grades Research Journal, 6,* 207-222.

94 Anstey, M., & Bull, G. (2006). *Teaching and learning multiliteracies: Changing times, changing literacies.* International Reading Association.

Sang, Y. (2017). Expanded territories of "literacy": New literacies and multiliteracies. *Journal of Education and Practice, 8*(8), 16-19.

Santori, D., & Smith, C. A. (2018). Teaching and learning with iPads to support dialogic construction of multiliteracies. *Middle School Journal, 49*(1), 24-31. https://doi.org/10.1080/00940771.2018.1398944

Tan, J. P. L., & McWilliam, E. (2009). From literacy to multiliteracies: Diverse learners and pedagogical practice. *Pedagogies: An International Journal, 4*(3), 213-225.

95 Phinney, J. S. (2008). Bridging identities and disciplines: Advances and challenges in understanding multiple identities. *New Directions for Child and Adolescent Development, 2008*(120), 97–109.

96 Harrison, L. M. (2017). Redefining intersectionality theory through the lens of African American young adolescent girls' racialized experiences. *Journal of Youth & Society, 49*(8), 1023-1039.

97 Phinney, J. S. (2008). Bridging identities and disciplines: Advances and challenges in understanding multiple identities. *New Directions for Child and Adolescent Development, 2008*(120), 97–109.

98 Cis-gender means that one's own gender identity corresponds with their birth sex.

99 Paris, D., & Alim, H. S. (Eds.). (2017). *Culturally sustaining pedagogies: Teaching and learning for justice in a changing world.* Teachers College Press.

100 Fergus, E. (2017). Confronting colorblindness. *Phi Delta Kappan, 98*(5), 30-35.

Liou, D. D., Leigh, P. R., Rotheram-Fuller, E., & Cutler, K. D. (2019). The Influence of teachers' colorblind expectations on the political, normative, and technical dimensions of educational reform. *International Journal of Educational Reform, 28*(1), 122-148.

101 Beucher, B. & Smith, A. (2019). #NoDAPL: Collaboratively designing culturally responsive curriculum. In K. M. Brinegar, L. M. Harrison, & E. Hurd (Eds.), *Equity & cultural responsiveness in the middle grades* (pp. 181-2106). Information Age Publishing.

102 Pacheco, M. B., & Smith, B. E. (2019). "Sounds funny" and making sense: Multimodal codemeshing as culturally sustaining pedagogy in an English-Centric classroom. In K. M. Brinegar, L. M. Harrison, & E. Hurd (Eds.), *Equity & cultural responsiveness in the middle grades* (pp. 93-112). Information Age Publishing.

103 Cochran-Smith, M. (2004). *Walking the road: Race, diversity, and social justice in teacher education.* Teachers College Press.

Gorski, P. C., & Swalwell, K. (2015). Equity literacy for all. *Educational leadership, 72*(6), 34-40.

104 Boyd, F. B., Causey, L. L., & Galda, L. (2015). Culturally diverse literature: Enriching variety in an era of Common Core State Standards. *The Reading Teacher, 68*(5), 378-387.

White, D. Y., Murray, E. C., & Brunaud-Vega, V. (2012). Discovering multicultural mathematics dispositions. *Journal of Urban Mathematics Education, 5*(1), 31-43.

105 Bousalis, R., & Furner, J. M. (2020). Linking middle school mathematics and social studies through immigration issues. *Middle School Journal, 51*(1), 19-28. https://doi.org/10.1080/00 940771.2019.1689777

Davis, C. L., & Hall, L. M. (2020). Spoken word performance as activism: Middle school poets challenge American racism. *Middle School Journal, 51*(2), 6-15. https://doi.org/ 10.1080/00940771.2019.1709256

Ellerbrock, C. R. & Vomvoridi-Ivanovic, E. (2019). A framework for responsive middle level mathematics teaching. In K. M. Brinegar, L. M. Harrison, & E. Hurd (Eds.), *Equity & cultural responsiveness in the middle grades* (pp.45-68). Information Age Publishing.

Gibbs grey, T. M. (2019). Illuminating the power of personal narrative writing to affirm the literacies and lives of Black youth. In K. M. Brinegar, L. M. Harrison, & E. Hurd (Eds.), *Equity & cultural responsiveness in the middle grades* (pp.45-68). Information Age Publishing.

Gutstein, E., & Peterson, B. (Eds.). (2005). *Rethinking mathematics: Teaching social justice by the numbers.* Rethinking Schools.

Harrison, L. M. (2015). Teaching social justice through mathematics: A self-study of bridging theory to practice. *Middle Grades Review, 1*(1), 1-13.

Zeidler, D. L., & Kahn, S. (2014). *It's debatable!: Using socioscientific issues to develop scientific literacy K-12.* NSTA press.

106 The Trevor Project. (2019). *National survey on LGBTQ mental health.* The Trevor Project.

Chandra-Mouli, V., Svanemyr, J., Amin, A., Fogstad, H., Say, L., Girard, F., & Temmerman, M. (2015). Twenty years after International Conference on Population and Development: Where are we with adolescent sexual and reproductive health and rights? *Journal of Adolescent Health, 56*(1), S1-S6.

Patton, G.C., et al., (2016). Our future: A Lancet commission on adolescent health and well-being. *The Lancet, 387*(10036), 2423-2478.

107 Dumith, S.C., Gigante, D.P., Domingues, M.R., & Kohl III, H.W. (2011). Physical activity change during adolescence: A systematic review and a pooled analysis. *International Journal of Epidemiology, 40*(3), 685-698.

108 Pan, C.-Y., Liu, C.-W., Chung, I. C., & Hsu, P.-J. (2015). Physical activity levels of adolescents with and without intellectual disabilities during physical education and recess. *Research in Developmental Disabilities, 36*, 579–586.

Zavacky, F., & Michael, S.L. (2017). Keeping recess in schools. *Journal of Physical Education, Recreation & Dance, 88*(5), 46-53

109 Zavacky, F., & Michael, S.L. (2017). Keeping recess in schools. *Journal of Physical Education, Recreation & Dance, 88*(5), 46-53

110 Panayiotou, M., Humphrey, N., & Wigelsworth, M. (2019). An empirical basis for linking social and emotional learning to academic performance. *Contemporary Educational Psychology, 56*, 193-204. https://www.sciencedirect.com/science/article/pii/S0361476X18303382

111 OECD. Social and emotional skills: Well-being connectedness and success. Retrieved from http://www.oecd.org/education/school/UPDATED%20Social%20and%20Emotional%20 Skills%20-%20Well-being,%20connectedness%20and%20success.pdf%20(website).pdf

112 See https://casel.org/

113 Henderson, B., & Strahan, D. (2014). *Research summary: Motivation: Understanding and responding to individual differences.* https://www.amle.org/TabId/270/ArtMID/888/ ArticleID/465/Motivation-Understanding-and-Responding-to-Individual-Differences.aspx

Knowles, T., & Brown, D. F. (2014). *What every middle school teacher should know.* Heinemann.

Pate, E. (2013). Academically excellent curriculum, instruction, and assessment. In P.G. Andrews (Ed.), *Research to guide practice in middle grades education* (pp. 165-186). Association for Middle Level Education.

114 Brinegar, K.M., Harrison, L.M., & Hurd, E. (Eds.) (2019). *Equity & cultural responsiveness in the middle grades.* Information Age Publications

González, N., Moll, L. C., & Amanti, C. (Eds.). (2006). *Funds of knowledge: Theorizing practices in households, communities, and classrooms.* Routledge.

Muhammad, G. (2020). *Cultivating genius: An equity framework for culturally and historically responsive literacy.* Scholastic.

Paris, D., & Alim, H. S. (Eds.). (2017). *Culturally sustaining pedagogies: Teaching and learning for justice in a changing world.* Teachers College Press.

115 Crosby, S. D., Howell, P., & Thomas, S. (2018). Social justice education through trauma-informed teaching. *Middle School Journal, 49*(4), 15-23. https://doi.org/10.1080/00940771.2018.1488470

Von Dohlen, H. B., Pinter, H. H., Winter, K. K., Ward, S., & Cody, C. (2019). Trauma-informed practices in a laboratory middle school. *Middle School Journal, 50*(4), 6-15. https://doi.org/10.1080/00940771.2019.1650549

116 Alley, K. M. (2019). Fostering middle school students' autonomy to support motivation and engagement. *Middle School Journal, 50*(3), 5-14. https://doi.org/10.1080/00940771.2019.1603801

117 Tomlinson, C. A. (2013). Differentiating instruction as a response to academic diversity. In P.G. Andrews (Ed.), *Research to guide practice in middle grades education* (pp. 165-186). Association for Middle Level Education.

118 Edwards, S. (2015). Active learning in the middle grades. *Middle School Journal, 46*(5), 26-32. https://doi.org/10.1080/00940771.2015.11461922

Christensen, R., & Knezek, G. (2018). Impact of middle school student energy monitoring activities on climate change beliefs and intentions. *School Science and Mathematics, 118*, 43-52. https://doi.org/10.1111/ssm.12257

Bishop, P., & Pflaum, S. (2005). Student perceptions of action, relevance, and pace. *Middle School Journal, 36*(4), 4-12. https://doi.org/10.1080/00940771.2005.11461489

119 Bishop, P.A., & Downes, J.M. (2019). *Optimizing teaching and learning in the middle grades.* (Remaking Middle School Working Paper series).Youth-Nex Center, University of Virginia. https://drive.google.com/file/d/1c009BXixwb4YjRkZlkR66GgjcwnVuLH4/view

120 Pate, E. (2013). Academically excellent curriculum, instruction, and assessment. In P.G. Andrews (Ed.), *Research to guide practice in middle grades education* (pp. 165-186). Association for Middle Level Education.

121 Bishop, P. A., Falk-Ross, F., Andrews, P. G., Cronenberg, S., Moran, C. M., & Weiler, C. S. (2018). Digital technologies in the middle grades. In S. B. Mertens & M. M. Caskey (Eds.), *Literature reviews in support of the middle level education research agenda* (pp. 10-14). Information Age Publishing.

Len-Ríos, M. E., Hughes, H. E., McKee, L. G., & Young, H. N. (2016). Early adolescents as publics: A national survey of teens with social media accounts, their media use preferences, parental mediation, and perceived Internet literacy. *Public Relations Review, 42*(1), 101-108.

122 Downes, J. M., & Bishop, P. A. (2015). The intersection between 1:1 laptop implementation and the characteristics of effective middle level schools. *RMLE Online, 38*(7), 1–16. https://doi.org/10.1080/19404476.2015.11462120

123 Becker, R., & Bishop, P. (2016). "Think bigger about science": Using Twitter for learning in the middle grades. *Middle School Journal, 47*(3), 4-16. https://doi.org/10.1080/00940771.2016.1135097

Bishop, P., & Downes, J. (2013). Technology in the middle grades classroom. In P.G. Andrews (Ed.). *Research to guide practice in middle grades education* (pp. 267-302). Association for Middle Level Education.

124 Downes, J. M., & Bishop, P. (2012). Educators engage digital natives and learn from their experiences with technology: Integrating technology engages students in their learning. *Middle School Journal, 43*(5), 6-15. https://doi.org/10.1080/00940771.2012.11461824

125 Wenzel, A., & Carano, K.T. (2015). *Research summary: Social media for middle level classrooms.* Association for Middle Level Education. http://www.amle.org/TabId/270/artmid/888/articleid/553/Social-Media-for-Middle-Level-Classrooms.aspx

126 Damon, M., Menon, J., & Bronk, C. (2003). The development of purpose during adolescence. *Applied Developmental Science, 7*(3), 119-128.

127 Farber, K., & Bishop, P. (2018). Service learning in the middle grades: Learning by doing and caring. *Research in Middle Level Education Online, 41*(2), 1-15. https://doi.org/10.1080/19404476.2017.1415600

128 Williams, J., Mims, L., & Johnson, H. (2019). *Young adolescent development* (Remaking Middle School Working Paper series).Youth-Nex Center, University of Virginia. https://drive.google.com/file/d/1pY5hM18aKBSDCWxYpx4XnxasMKUeyyy-/view

129 AIR. Study of deeper learning: Opportunities and outcomes. https://www.air.org/project/study-deeper-learning-opportunities-and-outcomes

130 Williams, J., Mims, L., & Johnson, H. (2019). *Young adolescent development* (Remaking Middle School Working Paper series).Youth-Nex Center, University of Virginia. https://drive.google.com/file/d/1pY5hM18aKBSDCWxYpx4XnxasMKUeyyy-/view

131 Wall, A., Massey, D., & Vaughn, M. (2018). *Research summary: Student agency.* Association for Middle Level Education. http://www.amle.org/TabId/270/artmid/888/articleid/995/Student-Agency.aspx

132 Beane, J.A. (1993). *A middle school curriculum: From rhetoric to reality* (2nd ed.). National Middle School Association.

Beane, J. A. (1997). *Curriculum integration: Designing the core of democratic education.* Teachers College Press.

133 Beane, J.A. (1993). *A middle school curriculum: From rhetoric to reality* (2nd ed.). National Middle School Association.

Beane, J. A. (1997). *Curriculum integration: Designing the core of democratic education.* Teachers College Press.

134 Biddle, C., & Mitra, D. (2015). Implementing middle school youth-adult partnerships: A study of two programs focused on social change," *Middle Grades Review, 1*(2), Article 6. https://scholarworks.uvm.edu/mgreview/vol1/iss2/6

135 Bishop, P.A., Downes, J.M., & Farber, K. (2019). *Personalized learning in the middle grades.* Harvard Education Press.

136 Gonell, E., Smith, L. C., Garnett, B., & Clements, E. (2020). Practicing youth participatory action research for school equity: A pedagogical model. Action Research. https://doi.org/10.1177/1476750319894052

Nelson, E., & Bishop, P. (2013). Students as action research partners: A New Zealand example. *Middle School Journal, 45*(2), 19-26. https://doi.org/10.1080/00940771.2013.11461883

137 Bishop, P.A., Downes, J.M., & Farber, K. (2019). *Personalized learning in the middle grades.* Harvard Education Press.

138 Bishop, P.A., & Downes, J.M. (2019). *Optimizing teaching and learning in the middle grades.* (Remaking Middle School Working Paper series).Youth-Nex Center, University of Virginia. https://drive.google.com/file/d/1c009BXixwb4YjRkZlkR66GgjcwnVuLH4/view

139 Strahan, D., & Rogers, C. (2012). *Research summary: Formative assessment practices in successful middle level classrooms.* Association for Middle Level Education. http://www.amle.org/Publications/ResearchSummary/TabId/622/ArtMID/2112/ArticleID/108/Formative-Assessment-Practices.aspx

Capraro, R. M., Roe, M. F., Caskey, M. M., Strahan, D., Bishop, P.A., Weiss, C. C., & Swanson, K. W. (2011). *Research summary: Assessment.* Association for Middle Level Education. http://www.amle.org/TabId/270/ArtMID/888/ArticleID/309/Research-Summary-Assessment.aspx

140 National Academies of Sciences, Engineering, and Medicine. (2019). *The promise of adolescence: Realizing opportunity for all youth.* The National Academies Press. https://doi.org/10.17226/25388.

141 Darling-Hammond, L., Friedlaender, D., & Snyder, J. (2014). *Student-centered schools: Policy supports for closing the opportunity gap.* Stanford Center for Opportunity Policy in Education. https://edpolicy.stanford.edu/sites/default/files/scope-pub-student-centered-policy.pdf

142 Brookhart, S. M., & Moss, C. M. (2014). Learning targets on parade. *Educational Leadership, 72*(7), 28–33.

Brookhart, S. M., & Moss, C. M. (2012). *Learning targets: Helping students aim for understanding in today's lesson.* Association for Supervision and Curriculum Development.

143 Baker, B. D. (2014). *America's most financially disadvantaged school districts and how they got that way: How state and local governance causes school funding disparities.* Center for American Progress.

Card, D., & Giuliano, L. (2016). Universal screening increases the representation of low-income and minority students in gifted education. *Proceedings of the National Academy of Sciences, 113*(48), 13678-13683.

Carter Andrews, D. J., & Gutwein, M. (2020). Middle school students' experiences with inequitable discipline practices in school: The elusive quest for cultural responsiveness. *Middle School Journal, 51*(1), 29-38. https://doi.org/10.1080/00940771.2019.1689778

Gibbs-Grey, T., & Harrison, L.M., (in press). Call me worthy: Utilizing storytelling to reclaim narratives about Black middle school girls experiencing inequitable school discipline. *Equity & Excellence in Education*

Walker, B. L. T. (2020). "Loud, proud, and love a crowd:" African American girls and school discipline practices. *Middle School Journal, 51*(1), 12-18. https://doi.org/10.1080/00940771.2019.1689776

Wright, B. L., Ford, D. Y., & Young, J. L. (2017). Ignorance or indifference? Seeking excellence and equity for under-represented students of color in gifted education. *Global Education Review, 4*(1), 45-60.

144 Carter Andrews, D. J., & Gutwein, M. (2020). Middle school students' experiences with inequitable discipline practices in school: The elusive quest for cultural responsiveness. *Middle School Journal, 51*(1), 29-38. https://doi.org/10.1080/00940771.2019.1689778

Downing. B. (2019). Middle (mis)management: Staff sanctioned victimization in the middle grades. In K. M. Brinegar, L. M. Harrison, & E. Hurd (Eds.), *Equity & cultural responsiveness in the middle grades* (pp. 113-131). Information Age Publishing.

Hanson, K. L., & Connor, L. (2018). Eating on schooldays and non-schooldays among children at risk for food insecurity: Implications for weekend food backpack programs. *Journal of Hunger & Environmental Nutrition, 13*(3), 322-334.

Marx, R. A., & Kettrey, H. H. (2016). Gay-Straight Alliances are associated with lower levels of school-based victimization of LGBTQ+ youth: A systematic review and meta-analysis. *Journal of Youth and Adolescence, 45*(7), 1269-1282.

Nojan, S. (2020). Why ethnic studies? Building critical consciousness among middle school students. *Middle School Journal, 51*(2), 25–35. https://doi.org/10.1080/00940771.2019.1709259

145 Khalifa, M. A. (2018). *Culturally responsive school leadership.* Harvard Education Press.

146 Please see sources listed for why it is important and strategies to recruit racially diverse teachers including in predominantly White schools and districts.

Carver-Thomas, D. (2018). *Diversifying the teaching profession: How to recruit and retain teachers of color.* Learning Policy Institute. https://learningpolicyinstitute.org/product/diversifying-teaching-profession-report#:~:text=Including%20teachers%20o f%20color%20 in,their%20first%20years%20of%20teaching

Carver-Thomas, D. (2017). *Diversifying the field: Barriers to recruiting and retaining teachers of color and how to overcome them.* Literature Review. Retrieved from https://files.eric.ed.gov/fulltext/ED582730.pdf

9 Strategies for Recruiting, Hiring, and Retaining Diverse Teachers. https://ies.ed.gov/ncee/edlabs/regions/northwest/pdf/teacher-attrition.pdf

147 Johnson, R. S. (2002). *Using data to close the achievement gap: How to measure equity in our schools.* Corwin Press.

Losen, D., & Skiba, R. (2010). *Suspended education: Urban middle schools in crisis.* Southern Poverty Law Center

148 Gale, J.J., & Bishop, P.A. (2014). The work of effective middle grades principals: Responsiveness and relationships. *RMLE Online, 37*(9), 1-23. https://doi.org/10.1080/19404476.2014.11462112

Anfara, V. A., Jr. , Pate, P. E., Caskey, M. M., Andrews, G., Daniel, L. G., Mertens, S. B., & Muir, M. (2008). *Research summary: Courageous, collaborative leadership.* Association for Middle Level Education. https://www.amle.org/Portals/0/pdf/research_summaries/Courageous_Leadership.pdf

149 Allensworth, E.M., & Hart, H. (2018). *How do principals influence student achievement?* University of Chicago Consortium on School Research.

150 ibid

151 Donohoo, J., Hattie, J., & Eells, R. (2018). The power of collective efficacy. *Educational Leadership, 75*(6), 40-44.

152 Allensworth, E.M., & Hart, H. (2018). *How do principals influence student achievement?* University of Chicago Consortium on School Research.

153 Darling-Hammond, L., Hyler, M. E., Gardner, M. (2017). *Effective teacher professional development.* Learning Policy Institute.

Bickmore, D.L. (2014). *Research summary: Professional learning and professional development in the middle grades.* Association for Middle Level Education. Retrieved from http://www.amle.org/TabId/622/ArtMID/2112/ArticleID/466/Professional-Learning-and-Professional-Development-in-the-Middle-Grades.aspx

154 Fullan, M., & Quinn, J. (2016). *Coherence making: How leaders cultivate the pathway for school and system change with a shared process.* https://www.scoe.org/files/Fullan_Quinn.pdf

Reeves, D.B. (2010). *Transforming professional development into student results.* ASCD.

155 Kiefer, S.M.; Ellerbrock, C.R. (2012). Caring and fun: Fostering an adolescent-centered community within an interdisciplinary team. *Middle Grades Research Journal, 7*(3), 1–17.

Wallace, J.J. (2007). Effects of interdisciplinary teaching team configuration upon the social bonding of middle school students. *RMLE. Online, 30*(5), 1–18. https://doi.org/10.1080/19404476.2007.11462038

Ellerbrock, C.R.; Kiefer, S.M. (2013).The interplay between adolescent needs and secondary school structures: Fostering developmentally responsive middle and high school environments across the transition. *High School Journal, 96*, 170–194.

Boyer, S. J., & Bishop, P. A. (2004). Young adolescent voices: Students' perceptions of interdisciplinary teaming. *RMLE Online, 28*(1). https://www.tandfonline.com/doi/abs/10.1080/19404476.2004.11658176

156 Wilcox, K.C., & Angelis, J.I. (2007). *What makes middle schools work: A report on best practices in New York state middle schools.* University at Albany.

Flowers, N., Mertens, S.B., & Mulhall, P.F. (2007). *Applying current middle grades research to improve classrooms and schools.* National Middle School Association.

Flowers, N., Mertens, S.B., & Mulhall, P.F. (2003). Lessons learned from more than a decade of middle grades research. *Middle School Journal, 35*(2), 55–59. https://doi.org/10.1080/19404476.2007.11462038

Robbins, C., & Searby, L.. (2013). Exploring parental involvement strategies utilized by middle school interdisciplinary teams. *School Community Journal, 23*(2), 113-136.

Steffes, B., & Valentine, J. (1996). The relationship between organizational characteristics and expected benefits in interdisciplinary teams. *Research in Middle Level Education Quarterly, 19*(4), 83-106.

157 Wallace, J.J. (2007). Effects of interdisciplinary teaching team configuration upon the social bonding of middle school students. *RMLE. Online, 30*(5), 1–18. https://doi.org/10.1080/19404476.2007.11462038

Hill, P.W., & Russell, V.J. (1999). Systemic whole school reform of the middle years of schooling. In R.J. Bosker, P.M. Creemers, & S. Stringfield (Eds), *Enhancing educational excellence, equity and efficiency* (pp. 167-196). Klewer Academic Publishing.

Flowers, N., Mertens, S.B., & Mulhall, P.F. (2000). How teaming influences classroom practices. *Middle School Journal, 32*(2), 52–59. https://doi.org/10.1080/00940771.2000.11495267

Flowers, N., Mertens, S.B., & Mulhall, P.F. (2000). What makes interdisciplinary teams effective. *Middle School Journal, 31*(4), 53–56. https://doi.org/10.1080/00940771.2000.11494640

158 Strahan, D., & Hedt, M. (2009). Teaching and teaming more responsively: Case studies in professional growth at the middle level. *Research in Middle Level Education Online, 32*(8), 1–14.

159 Dever, R., & Lash, M.J. (2013). Using common planning time to foster professional learning. *Middle School Journal, 45*(1), 12-17. https://doi.org/10.1080/00940771.2013.11461877

Cook, C.M., & Faulkner, S.A. (2010). The use of common planning time: A case study of two Kentucky Schools to Watch. *RMLE Online, 34*(2), 1-12. https://doi.org/10.1080/19404476.2010.11462075

160 Umansky, I. M. (2016). Leveled and exclusionary tracking: English learners' access to academic content in middle school. *American Educational Research Journal, 53*(6), 1792–1833. https://doi.org/10.3102/0002831216675404

Kangas, S. E. N., & Cook, M. (2020). Academic tracking of English learners with disabilities in middle school. *American Educational Research Journal.* https://doi.org/10.3102/0002831220915702

Stanley, D., & Venzant Chambers, T.T. (2018). Tracking myself: African American high school students talk about the effects of curricular differentiation. *International Journal of Education Policy & Leadership 13*(1). http://journals.sfu.ca/ijepl/index.php/ijepl/article/view/748

Hamilton, R., McCoach, D. B., Tutwiler, M.S., Siegle, D., Gubbins, E.J., Callahan, C.M., Brodersen, A. V., & Mun, R.U. (2018). Disentangling the roles of institutional and individual poverty in the identification of gifted students. *Gifted Child Quarterly, 62*(1). https://journals.sagepub.com/doi/full/10.1177/0016986217738053

Grissom, J.A., & Redding, C. (2016). Discretion and disproportionality: Explaining the underrepresentation of high-achieving students of color in gifted programs. *AERA Open, 2*(1), 1–25. https://journals.sagepub.com/doi/pdf/10.1177/2332858415622175

161 Characteristics and implications were retrieved from these sources

Caskey, M. M., & Anfara, Jr., V. A. (2014). *Research summary: Developmental characteristics of young adolescents.* Association for Middle Level Education. http://www.amle.org/BrowsebyTopic/WhatsNew/WNDet.aspx?ArtMID=888& ArticleID=455

Kellough, R. D., & Kellough, N. G. (2008). *Teaching young adolescents: Methods and resources for middle grades teaching* (5th ed.). Pearson.

National Academies of Sciences, Engineering, and Medicine. (2019). The promise of adolescence: Realizing opportunity for all youth. The National Academies Press. https://doi.org/10.17226/25388

Powell, S. D. (2014). *Introduction to middle school* (3rd ed.). Pearson.

Russell, S. T., & Fish, J. N. (2017). Mental health in lesbian, gay, bisexual, and transgender (LGBT) youth. *Annual Review of Clinical Psychology, 12*, 465–487.

Scales, P.C. (2010). Characteristics of young adolescents. In *This we believe: Keys to Educating young adolescents* (pp. 53–62). National Middle School Association.

162 Jackson, A., & Davis, G. A. (2000). *Turning points 2000: Educating adolescents in the 21st century.* Teachers College Press

163 Smith, T., & McEwin, K. (2011). *The legacy of middle school leaders in their own words.* Information Age.

Schaefer, M. B., Malu, K. F., & Yoon, B. (2016). An historical overview of the middle school movement, 1963–2015. *RMLE Online, 35*(5),1-27. https://doi.org/10.1080/19404476.2016.1165036

164 Harrison, L. M., Hurd, E., & Brinegar, K. M. (2019). Exploring the convergence of developmentalism and cultural responsiveness. In K. M. Brinegar, L. M. Harrison, & E. Hurd (Eds.), *Equity & cultural responsiveness in the middle grades* (pp. 3-23). Information Age Publishing.

Kennedy-Lewis, B., Brinegar, K., Hurd, E., & Harrison, L. M., (2016) Synthesizing middle grades research on cultural responsiveness: The importance of a shared conceptual framework, *Middle Grades Review, 2*(3), 1-19

Hughes, H. (2012). Always becoming never enough: Middle school girls talk back. In M. Vagle (Ed.), *Not a stage! A critical reconceptualization of young adolescent education* (pp. 93-118). Peter Lang.

Lesko, N. (2001). *Act your age: A cultural construction of adolescence.* Routledge.

Vagle, M. D. (2012). Introduction: Being a bit disruptive. In M. D. Vagle (Ed.), *Not a stage! A critical re-conception of young adolescent education* (pp. 1–9). Peter Lang.

165 National Academies of Sciences, Engineering, and Medicine (2019). *The promise of adolescence: Realizing opportunity for all youth.* The National Academies Press. https://doi.org/10.17226/25388.

166 Lesko, N. (2001). *Act your age: A cultural construction of adolescence.* Routledge.

Scales, P. C. (2010). Characteristics of young adolescents. In *This we believe: Keys to Educating young adolescents* (pp. 53–62). National Middle School Association.

167 Vagle, M.D. & Leitl, T. (2019). Missed Opportunities, No More. In K. M. Brinegar, L. M. Harrison, & E. Hurd(Eds.), *Equity & cultural responsiveness in the middle grades* (pp. 23-45). Information Age Publishing

168 Blake, J. J., & Epstein, R. (2019). Listening to Black Women and Girls: Lived Experiences of Adultification Bias (pp. 1–18). Georgetown Law Center on Poverty and Inequality.

169 Epstein, R., Blake, J., González, T. (2017). *Girlhood interrupted: The erasure of Black girls' childhood.* Center on Poverty and Inequality. http://www.law.georgetown.edu/academics/centers-institutes/poverty-inequality/upload/girlhood-interrupted.pdf

170 Scales, P. C. (2010). Characteristics of young adolescents. In *This we believe: Keys to Educating young adolescents* (pp. 53–62). National Middle School Association.

171 Brinegar, K. (2015). A content analysis of four peer-reviewed middle grades publications: Are we really paying attention to every young adolescent? *Middle Grades Review, 1*(1), 1–8. Retrieved from https://files.eric.ed.gov/fulltext/EJ1154860.pdf

National Academies of Sciences, Engineering, and Medicine. (2019). *The promise of adolescence: Realizing opportunity for all youth.* The National Academies Press. https://doi.org/10.17226/25388.

172 Anderson, R. E., McKenny, M. C., & Stevenson, H. C. (2019). EMBRace: Developing a racial socialization intervention to reduce racial stress and enhance racial coping among Black parents and adolescents. *Family Process, 58*(1), 53-67.

Comas-Díaz, L., Hall, G. N., & Neville, H. A. (2019). Racial trauma: Theory, research, and healing: Introduction to the special issue. *American Psychologist, 74*(1), 1.

Hardy, K. V. (2013). Healing the hidden wounds of racial trauma. *Reclaiming Children and Youth, 22*(1), 24.

173 Alvarez, A., Milner, H. R., & Delale-O'Connor, L. (2016). Race, trauma, and education: What educators need to know. In T. Husband (Ed.), *But I don't see color: The perils, practices, and possibilities of antiracist education* (pp. 27-40). Brill Sense.

Henderson, D. X., Walker, L., Barnes, R. R., Lunsford, A., Edwards, C., & Clark, C. (2019). A framework for race-related trauma in the public education system and implications on health for Black youth. *Journal of School Health, 89*(11), 926-933.

174 National Child Traumatic Stress Network, Justice Consortium, Schools Committee, and Culture Consortium. (2017). *Addressing race and trauma in the classroom: A resource for educators.* National Center for Child Traumatic Stress. https://www.nctsn.org/sites/default/files/resources/addressing_race_and_trauma_in_the_classroom_educators.pdf

175 Hardy, K. V. (2013). Healing the hidden wounds of racial trauma. *Reclaiming Children and Youth, 22*(1), 24.

Silverman, J., & Mee, M. (2019). Community circles: Mitigating the impact of trauma on the middle school student. *Middle School Journal, 50*(4), 35-41. https://doi.org/10.1080/00940771.2019.1650547

176 Martin, F., Wang, C., Petty, T., Wang, W., & Wilkins, P. (2018). Middle school students' social media use. *Journal of Educational Technology & Society, 21*(1), 213-224.

177 Silverman, J., & Mee, M. (2019). Community circles: Mitigating the impact of trauma on the middle school student. *Middle School Journal, 50*(4), 35-41. https://doi.org/10.1080/00940771.2019.1650547

About the Association for Middle Level Education

For nearly 50 years, the Association for Middle Level Education (AMLE) has been a voice for those committed to the educational and developmental needs of students ages 10 to 15. AMLE helps middle grades educators reach every student, grow professionally, and create great schools. AMLE members are principals, teachers, counselors, school district personnel, professors, college students, parents, and community leaders across the United States and around the world. Our network of affiliate organizations in the United States, Canada, Europe, and Australia strengthens our outreach to the regional, state, provincial, and local levels.

AMLE provides thought leadership, professional development, research, books, articles, and other services and resources to assist educators on an ongoing basis. Our annual conference and leadership institutes offer the largest and most comprehensive professional learning opportunities for middle grades educators.

If you are interested in the education and well-being of students in the middle grades, we welcome you to join us.

Web — www.amle.org

Twitter — @AMLE

Facebook — facebook.com/amle.org

Instagram — amleorg